FORD'S THEATRE
AND THE
LINCOLN ASSASSINATION

Eastern National
Serving the Visitors to America's
National Parks and Other Public Trusts

FORD'S THEATRE AND THE LINCOLN ASSASSINATION
Project manager: Michael Metallo
Author: Victoria Grieve
Editor: Paula Degen
Contributors: Sandra Walia; National Park Service: Donna Donaldson, Robert Fudge, Suzanne Kelley,
     Michael Maione, Melanie Spoo
Cover and interior book design: Barbara Cross
Image research: Barbara Cross
Project coordinator: Eve Hess
Digital imaging: Gabe Metallo, Robert Hess

Library of Congress Number: 00-103870
ISBN: 1-59091-040-0
Printed in the United States of America.

Foreword

by Michael Beschloss

Few moments in the American past do we remember so vividly that it seems as if we were there. The fateful burst of gunfire on Friday, April 14, 1865, was one of them. This book takes you into the heart of what has been called "the most terrible night in American history."

As Carl Sandburg wrote, "The moment of high fate was not seen by the theater audience. Only one man saw that moment.... Softly he had opened the door and stepped toward his prey, in his right hand a one-shot brass derringer pistol.... For Abraham Lincoln it was lights out, good night, farewell and a long farewell to the good earth and its trees, its enjoyable companions, and the Union of States and the world Family of Man he had loved."

Lincoln's assassination at Ford's Theatre still haunts our imagination almost a century and a half later. The greatest President in American history was struck down at the climax of our bloodiest war, the victim of our first Presidential murder. By telegraph, Americans across the country learned the news almost instantaneously and reacted to Lincoln's passing with the most widespread outpouring of grief the young nation had ever seen.

With Lincoln removed from the scene, the American Presidency passed to an unknown Southerner, Andrew Johnson, who had his own ideas about how to bind up the nation's wounds after the end of the Civil War. Today, we still wonder how the history of North and South and the African-American struggle for equal rights might have been different had Abraham Lincoln lived.

As with the assassination of John Kennedy, scholars cannot agree on who exactly was behind Lincoln's murder. Was the culprit merely John Wilkes Booth and his hapless small band of co-plotters, or did the plot extend far beyond them to include high-ranking members of the United States or Confederate governments?

This volume on the Lincoln assassination is a splendid introduction to one of the most important episodes in the American story. You will read about Ford's Theatre, how it was built and by whom; Lincoln himself and earlier plots against his life; the historical context of April 1865; Booth, his politics, his rage for fame, and his strange collaborators; the commotion in the Presidential Box, the death of a President, and the national trauma; the assassin's escape and capture, and what happened in the end to all of the players in the drama. The story culminates in the triumphant revival of Ford's Theatre as both a national historic treasure and a world-class theater—a tribute to our American instinct to preserve and cherish the monuments of even the darkest moments of our past.

Historian Michael Beschloss is now at work on a major history of Abraham Lincoln's assassination. He has been fascinated by Lincoln since childhood visits to Lincoln sites in Illinois and Ford's Theatre, in Washington, D.C. Among his other books are *The Johnson White House Tapes* and *The Crisis Years: Kennedy and Khrushchev, 1960-1963.*

Photographers of the Mathew Brady Studio created a photographic record of the Civil War. Here, photographer Alexander Gardner captured President Lincoln's visit to the headquarters of the Army of the Potomac at the Antietam battlefield, October 3, 1862.

Introduction

On the night of April 14, 1865, the greatest cast of characters yet assembled at Ford's Theatre would gather for the explosive climax of a larger drama, the American Civil War. President Abraham Lincoln and actor John Wilkes Booth were destined to star in the leading roles in the tragedy that night, but many other players and events brought them to that stage.

The scene was a divided nation at war. The cast list included Confederate spies and an ambitious theater owner, scheming conspirators, and unwitting accomplices. The long-awaited end to the war brought them to Ford's Theatre with President Lincoln, his wife Mary, and approximately 1,700 spectators that night. In an ironic twist of fate, a frivolous comedy was interrupted when real life drama stole the show. Although the audience came to see a popular lightweight farce, it witnessed instead the tragic assassination of President Abraham Lincoln.

In retrospect, the Lincoln assassination reads like the grand finale of an extraordinary national play, with a colorful array of characters caught up in the turmoil of war and Reconstruction. It is somehow fitting that this historic drama was performed at Ford's Theatre, an institution in Washington, D.C., theater circles. Since its opening as Ford's Atheneum at the onset of the Civil War, the theater seemed to run opposite the current of the times. Rebuilt against great odds during the hardest times of the war in 1863, the theater would fall into infamy at the jubilant end of the hostilities a year and a half later.

Since that time, the playhouse has survived a structural collapse and four modifications. Today, as a national historic site, Ford's Theatre is a place of solemn remembrance for the legendary President who was shot there and a dynamic, modern, living theater for new generations.

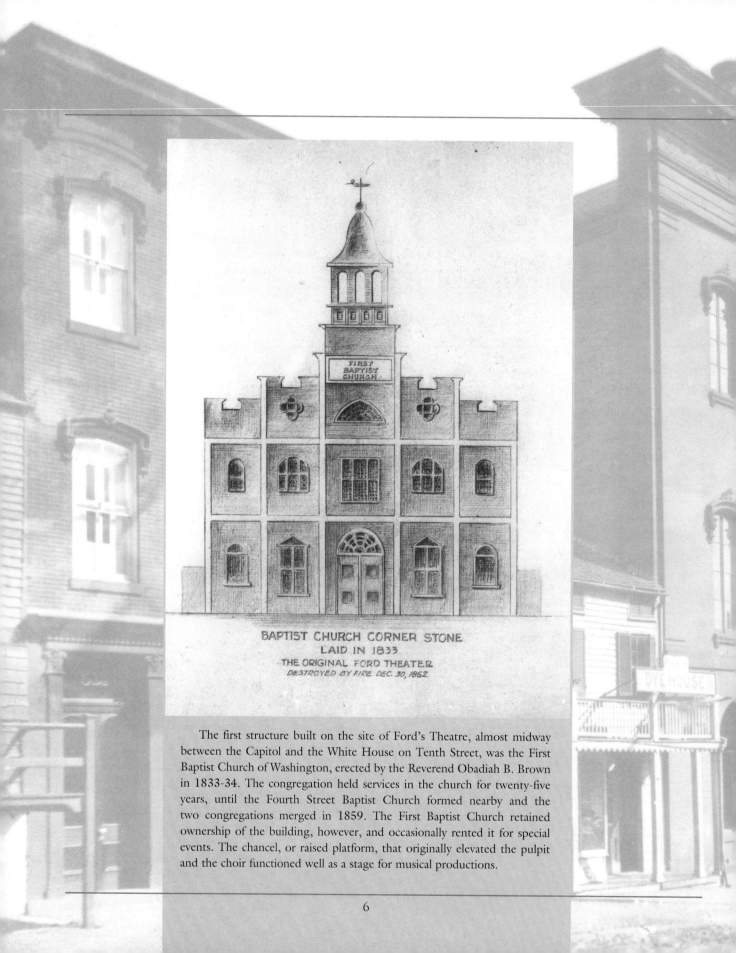

FIRST
BAPTIST
CHURCH

BAPTIST CHURCH CORNER STONE
LAID IN 1833
THE ORIGINAL FORD THEATER
DESTROYED BY FIRE DEC. 30, 1862

The first structure built on the site of Ford's Theatre, almost midway between the Capitol and the White House on Tenth Street, was the First Baptist Church of Washington, erected by the Reverend Obadiah B. Brown in 1833-34. The congregation held services in the church for twenty-five years, until the Fourth Street Baptist Church formed nearby and the two congregations merged in 1859. The First Baptist Church retained ownership of the building, however, and occasionally rented it for special events. The chancel, or raised platform, that originally elevated the pulpit and the choir functioned well as a stage for musical productions.

Setting the Stage

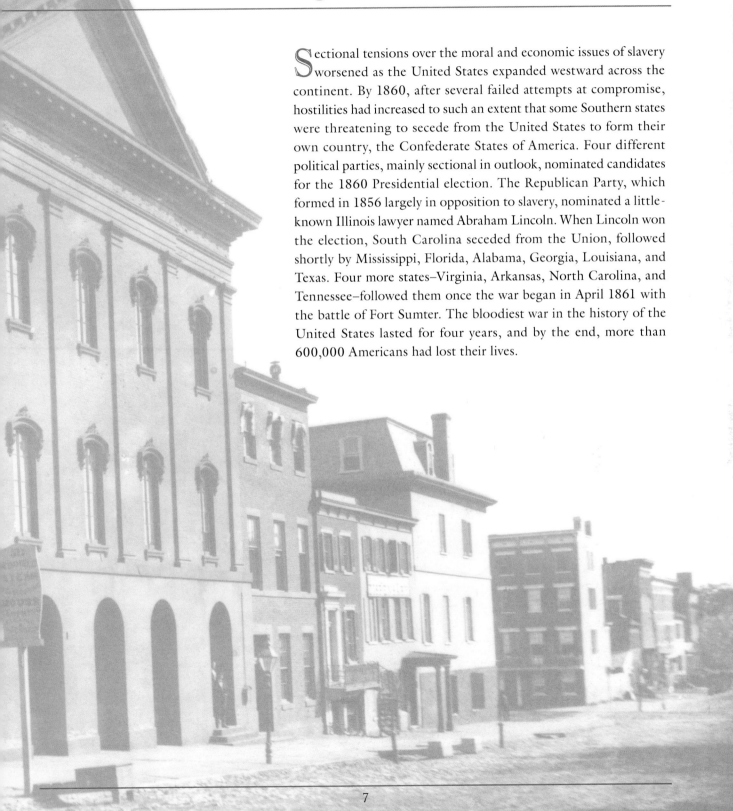

Sectional tensions over the moral and economic issues of slavery worsened as the United States expanded westward across the continent. By 1860, after several failed attempts at compromise, hostilities had increased to such an extent that some Southern states were threatening to secede from the United States to form their own country, the Confederate States of America. Four different political parties, mainly sectional in outlook, nominated candidates for the 1860 Presidential election. The Republican Party, which formed in 1856 largely in opposition to slavery, nominated a little-known Illinois lawyer named Abraham Lincoln. When Lincoln won the election, South Carolina seceded from the Union, followed shortly by Mississippi, Florida, Alabama, Georgia, Louisiana, and Texas. Four more states–Virginia, Arkansas, North Carolina, and Tennessee–followed them once the war began in April 1861 with the battle of Fort Sumter. The bloodiest war in the history of the United States lasted for four years, and by the end, more than 600,000 Americans had lost their lives.

Ford's Theatre presents

Understudies

For Charlie Anderson – Brian Sutherland*/Stephen F. Schmidt*; for Jacob/Engineer – Peter Boyer*; for James/Sam – Geoff Packard*; for Nathan /John/Drifter – Evan Casey*; for Henry/Lieutenant/Corporal – Timothy Dale Lewis*; for Robert – Zack Phillips; for Jenny/Anne – Tracy Lynn Olivera*; for Gabriel – Aaron Hilliard; for Reverend Byrd – Stephen F. Schmidt*; for Carol/Sergeant Johnson/Tinkham – Richard Frederick*; Male Swing/Confederate Sniper - Danny Tippett.*

Member, Actors' Equity Association, union of professional actors and stage managers.

Understudies never substitute for listed players unless a specific announcement is made at the time of the performance.

Additional Townspeople

CHERRY HARTH BAUMBUSCH

Cherry is a native Washingtonian and a graduate of Marymount University. For many years she has been a supernumerary actress at the Kennedy Center for The Washington National Opera, the American Ballet Theatre, The National Ballet of Canada and other organizations.

ANNA MARIE SELL

This production is Anna Marie's debut at Ford's Theatre. Regional credits: Cumberland Theatre: *Sound of Music* (Maria) and *Pippin* (Catherine); Wayside Theatre: *Hank Williams: Lost Highway* (Waitress), and *Nunsense Jamboree* (Amnesia). Upcoming: American Shakespeare Center: *Julius Caesar* (Calphurnia), *Midsummer...* (Hermia) and *Cyrano de Bergerac* (Roxane).

RACHEL ZAMPELLI

Favorite productions: Santa Clara University: *Streetcar...Desire* (Blanche Dubois), *Kiss Me Kate* (Lois Lane), *The Learned Ladies* (Philaminte) and *The King Stag* (Smeraldina). Recent credits: Riverside Theatre Works: *Grease* (Rizzo) and *Nunsense* (Sister Hubert); New Repertory Theatre: *Into the Woods* and *Romeo and Juliet*. Training: BA in theatre, Santa Clara University, 2004.

Program Notes

The musical *Shenandoah* is based on the 1965 film starring James Stewart as Charlie Anderson. James Lee Barrett, who wrote the screenplay, would eventually be credited with the book of the musical, along with director/producer Philip Rose and Peter Udell (who also wrote the lyrics). The team of Rose, Udell and composer Gary Geld had recently come off of the hit Broadway musical *Purlie* (1970), and were looking for a new project. According to Mr. Rose, "One day Peter came to my office and asked if I knew the Jimmy Stewart film *Shenandoah* (not a musical), which he had just seen on television. It took less than a minute for me to embrace Peter's idea and to go to the telephone and begin to make the required phone calls. One of my calls was to Jimmy Stewart offering him the lead in our musical. He responded with a lovely letter some weeks later, after reading our new musical script. He said our version was much better than the original, but he couldn't do it because he wasn't a good singer."

They found their lead performer in Broadway veteran John Cullum and *Shenandoah* opened at the Alvin Theatre on January 7, 1975. It ran for over two years and an astonishing 1,050 performances. It was nominated for six Tony Awards, winning two: Best Book of a Musical and Best Actor in a Musical (John Cullum). The musical was revived on Broadway in 1989, again with Mr. Rose directing and Mr. Cullum in the lead role.

The seed for the Ford's Theatre production was planted during an audition session for Ford's production of *Big River*, directed by Jeff Calhoun. After an actor performed a song from the show, Jeff turned to the room and said "That musical is never done. Am I the only one who likes it?" The answer, which came from a surprising source, was emphatically no: two weeks earlier, Producing Director Paul Tetreault had mentioned how *Shenandoah* was one of his favorite musicals and that he'd love to do a production of it some day – and that Ford's was the perfect venue. The director and producer soon began talking about the show, and the rest, as they say, is history. Mr. Calhoun worked with the authors and his team of collaborators (co-choreographer Chase Brock, Musical Director Steven Landau, designer Tobin Ost, lighting designer Michael Gilliam and associate director Coy Middlebrook), to strengthen and streamline the structure of the piece. Mr. Landau was engaged to write new orchestrations to give the musical a more contemporary feel and Mr. Ost designed sets that used the unique setting of Ford's Theatre to full advantage while allowing for a cinematic flow of the scenery. Rearranging scenes, distributing some songs to additional singers and cutting others altogether, Calhoun and his team worked to keep the story of the Anderson family firmly in focus. The result is a reinvented *Shenandoah* that audiences at Ford's are the first anywhere to experience. By re-imagining *Shenandoah*, Ford's Theatre honors the original while allowing its powerful resonances speak more clearly and passionately to today's audience.

President-Elect Lincoln

On the morning of February 11, 1861, despite a drizzling rain, a large crowd gathered at the Great Western Railway Station in Springfield, Illinois, to bid farewell to the friend, neighbor, lawyer, and politician who had lived and worked in the town for twenty-five years. The thin, lanky man towered over the assembly as he stood in the rain on the rear platform of his train and bid "an affectionate farewell" to his home and his neighbors, "not knowing when, or whether ever" he would return. Then the train pulled slowly out of the station under the watchful eyes of Abraham Lincoln's guards, bound for the Nation's Capital.

Lincoln's controversial election, the result of a four party split over the issues of slavery and states rights, ignited secession conventions throughout the Southern states. By the time Lincoln arrived in Washington, seven states had seceded from the Union, and four more ultimately would join them to form the Confederate States of America. The border states of Kentucky, Missouri, Maryland, and Delaware were hotbeds of protest and dissension, as unionists and secessionists fought for control over state legislatures and public opinion.

Civil War loomed over the nation like a black cloud. Lincoln and his family had been harassed with threats of violence and death since

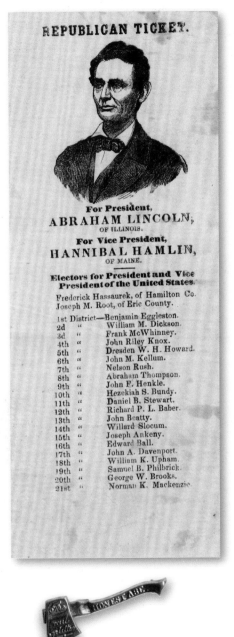

When Lincoln ran for office in 1860, a four-way split over the issue of slavery contributed to his controversial election. Campaign posters and pins showed pictures of Abraham Lincoln and Hannibal Hamlin (left). Above are the Republican ticket of 1860 and a campaign pin, "Honest Abe, The Railsplitter."

his election to the Presidency in November. Mindful of their safety, Lincoln insisted that his wife Mary and two young sons, Willie and Tad, travel separately.

The new President-elect was little known to his country, especially in the East, and Americans were eager to see the man who would lead the nation through the gathering storm. Lincoln stopped in all the major Northern cities to meet with governors, legislators, and the press, and to attend plays, concerts, and patriotic parades. He stopped in Columbus, Pittsburgh, and Cleveland, then in Westfield, New York. There, to the delight of the press, he kissed little Grace Bedell, who had written Lincoln during the campaign and suggested that he grow whiskers to look more presidential.

Lincoln spoke to enormous congregations in New York City on February 18, the same day Jefferson Davis, the senator from Mississippi just a few weeks earlier, was elected provisional president of the Confederacy at a convention in Montgomery, Alabama. And in Philadelphia, Lincoln raised an American flag over Independence Hall, reminding all Americans of their common past and their forefathers' commitment to democratic government.

"I shall not easily forget the first time I saw Abraham Lincoln. It must have been about the 18th or 19th of February, 1861 . . . . It was a pleasant spring afternoon, in New York city, as Lincoln arrived there from the West to stop a few hours and then pass on to Washington, to prepare for his inauguration. . . . there was much anxiety in certain quarters. Cautious persons had fear'd that there would be some outbreak, some marked indignity or insult to the President-elect on his passage through the city, for he posess'd no personal popularity in New York, and not much political. No such outbreak or insult, however, occurr'd. Only the silence of the crowd was very significant to those who were accustom'd to the usual demonstrations of New York in wild, tumultuous hurrahs. . . ."

excerpt from
"Memoranda During the War (1875-1876)"
WALT WHITMAN

Brass knuckles and eye shields used for protection by Lincoln's bodyguards are evidence of security concerns for the newly elected President. A special ticket (above) was issued to Capt. George Hargood, who accompanied Lincoln's inaugural train.

"On his way to Washington, his Illinois friends fearing danger, surround him and conceal him from his enemies."

Lincoln was lampooned in the press for his secret train ride through Baltimore. In later years, the President would not be so concerned with his personal safety.

As Lincoln's train pulled out of Harrisburg, Pennsylvania, bound for Washington, D.C., Lincoln's security detail and private detective Allan Pinkerton received word that an assassination attempt would be made by a mob of pro-secessionist "plug-uglies" in Baltimore. All telegraph lines were cut to prevent communication to and from the city. Lincoln's scheduled stop was canceled, and the train rolled quietly into Baltimore's station at 3:30 a.m. Lincoln and his guards waited a tense hour without incident for a connecting train, which the President-elect hurriedly boarded in the darkness and traveled on to Washington. Lincoln arrived in the Capital at 6 a.m. on February 23 and checked into the Willard Hotel on Pennsylvania Avenue, where he lived until after his inauguration.

The newspapers ran countless variations of Lincoln's secret passage through Baltimore, and the critical press had a field day mocking the cloak-and-dagger intrigue. One popular version described Lincoln as dressed in a Scotch plaid cap and a long military cloak; others clad him in women's clothing. The Southern press was merciless in its attacks on Lincoln. Political cartoons pictured the President dressed in various outrageous costumes, cowardly sneaking through the Baltimore train depot and fretting to his protectors. Lincoln's faithful bodyguard, Ward Hill Lamon, later wrote that Lincoln regretted his seeming overreaction to the warnings of his friends and security guards, fearing that he had damaged his reputation by succumbing to the rumors about his personal safety. In later years, the President would not be so careful.

The Lincoln Family

Abraham Lincoln

Abraham Lincoln was born on February 12, 1809, in a one-room log cabin on the Kentucky frontier. From his rough beginnings, Lincoln worked hard to educate himself, often staying up well into the night to read by the dying embers of the fire. As a boy he did not attend school regularly, working instead on his father's farm as he grew into a tall, wiry young man with a dark complexion and coarse black hair. Lincoln's quick wit and natural intelligence made him popular among his small town neighbors, and he soon became involved in politics, serving four terms in the state legislature. From there, Lincoln went on to serve in the U.S. House of Representatives. After three years of courtship, Lincoln married Mary Todd, a well-educated young woman from Kentucky, in 1842.

Although Lincoln lost his bid for the U.S. Senate to Democrat Stephen Douglas in 1858, their well-publicized debates captured the attention of Republican Party leaders. By 1860, Lincoln had made enough of a name for himself to be mentioned as a possible Presidential candidate for the party, yet was unknown enough not to have established an unsavory reputation with the public. His party nominated him, and in 1860, Abraham Lincoln became the sixteenth President of the United States of America at a most crucial time in its history.

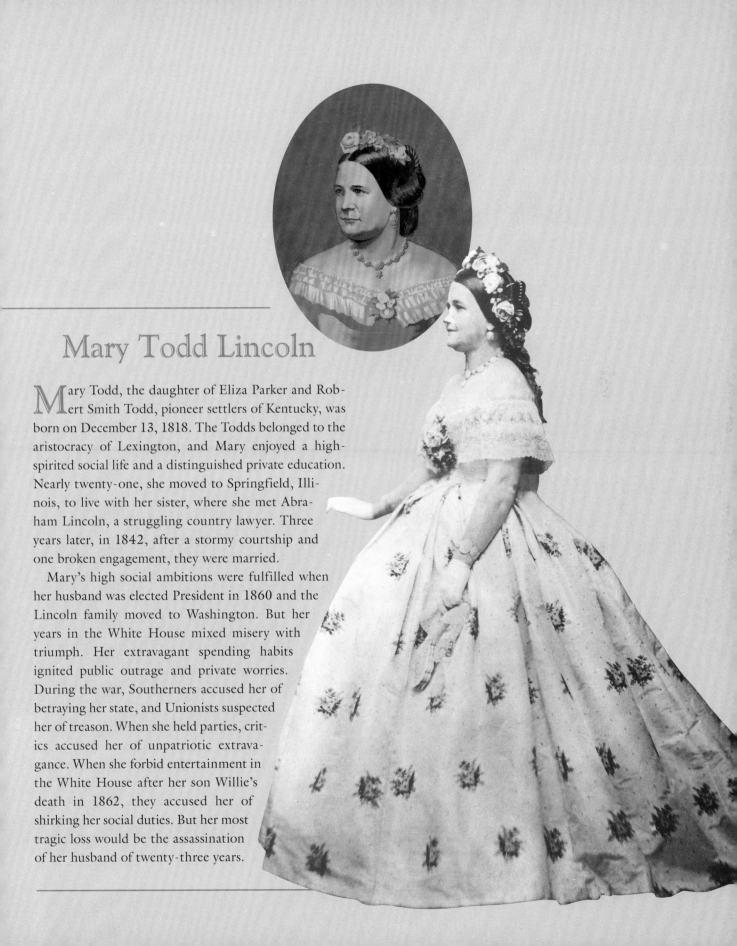

Mary Todd Lincoln

Mary Todd, the daughter of Eliza Parker and Robert Smith Todd, pioneer settlers of Kentucky, was born on December 13, 1818. The Todds belonged to the aristocracy of Lexington, and Mary enjoyed a high-spirited social life and a distinguished private education. Nearly twenty-one, she moved to Springfield, Illinois, to live with her sister, where she met Abraham Lincoln, a struggling country lawyer. Three years later, in 1842, after a stormy courtship and one broken engagement, they were married.

Mary's high social ambitions were fulfilled when her husband was elected President in 1860 and the Lincoln family moved to Washington. But her years in the White House mixed misery with triumph. Her extravagant spending habits ignited public outrage and private worries. During the war, Southerners accused her of betraying her state, and Unionists suspected her of treason. When she held parties, critics accused her of unpatriotic extravagance. When she forbid entertainment in the White House after her son Willie's death in 1862, they accused her of shirking her social duties. But her most tragic loss would be the assassination of her husband of twenty-three years.

This 1865 engraving, which is displayed in the Lincoln Museum at Ford's Theatre, was created by Adam Walter after President Abraham Lincoln was shot April 14, 1865. It soon became one of the most popular prints of the Lincoln family. Walter worked from individual photographs of the Lincolns and made a composite drawing of the family for the completed engraving. He included on the wall a portrait of Willie Lincoln, who died in 1862 in the White House, at the age of eleven.

The Lincoln Children

Mary Todd and Abraham Lincoln were married in Springfield, Illinois, on the evening of November 4, 1842. The couple had four sons, only one of whom, Robert, the first born, survived to adulthood. Their second son, Eddie, died in infancy on February 1, 1850.

Willie Lincoln, whom his mother described as "a very beautiful boy, with a most spiritual expression of face," died in the White House on February 20, 1862, at the age of eleven. The child's death devastated his parents, neither of whom ever recovered completely from the loss.

After Willie's untimely death, the Lincolns indulged their youngest son Tad. Named for Lincoln's father Thomas, Tad was born with a cleft palate that resulted in a lisp. Much to the dismay of Lincoln's Cabinet, Tad often burst into meetings, once demanding a Presidential pardon for his doll Jack. He raised funds for the Sanitary Commission by charging a 5 cent toll to use the White House stairs, and entertained friends by harnessing a dining chair to his two pet goats, Nanny and Nanko. Tad died on July 15, 1871, at the age of eighteen, about six years after the assassination of his father.

The Lincolns' oldest son, Robert, joined General Grant's staff during the Civil War and witnessed the surrender of Robert E. Lee and the Army of Northern Virginia at Appomattox Court House on April 9, 1865. He went on to become a successful lawyer, businessman, and government official. In 1922, he attended the dedication of the Lincoln Memorial in Washington, built in honor of his father. Robert Lincoln died on July 26, 1926, just a few days before his eighty-third birthday. He is buried in Arlington National Cemetery.

Thomas "Tad" Lincoln

Willie Lincoln

Robert Lincoln

Inauguration

Shortly before noon on a bleak and chilly March 4, 1861, President-elect Lincoln rode to the Capitol with outgoing President James Buchanan. A closely formed heavy guard surrounded the open carriage as they rode down Pennsylvania Avenue. With military sharpshooters stationed on rooftops and armed guards posted at regular intervals, Lincoln read his inaugural address slowly and solemnly from the East Portico before a crowd of 30,000 spectators. In a vain striving for peaceful reconciliation, Lincoln reassured Southerners that their property was safe and asserted that "the Union is perpetual." He addressed himself to all Southerners, but singled out "persons who seek to destroy the Union…. In your hands, my dissatisfied countrymen," he told them, "and not in mine, is the momentous issue of Civil War. You have no oath registered in Heaven to destroy the government, while I shall have the most solemn one to preserve, protect and defend it." Chief Justice Roger B. Taney administered the oath of office and thunderous cannon salutes boomed over the Capital City, foreshadowing the terrible struggle ahead.

Throngs of curious spectators climbed trees, sat on rooftops, and lined Pennsylvania Avenue from the White House to the unfinished Capitol, where Abraham Lincoln would be sworn in as the sixteenth President of the United States.

Washington, D.C., in 1861

Newcomers to the city were generally dismayed with the appearance of the Nation's Capital. Some official public structures, such as the Executive Mansion and the Treasury building, were impressive enough, but blocks of stone and scaffolding surrounded the unfinished Capitol building on the hill. The lower half of Pennsylvania Avenue was but a stretch of mud or dust, depending on the weather, and the broken-off stub of the Washington Monument rose above the foul-smelling tidal marshes of the Potomac River. During the summer, the heat and humidity were oppressive, and winters were bitter cold. Regardless, throngs of political hopefuls and military men, accompanied by newspaper correspondents and entertainers, filled the city's hotels and boardinghouses and crowded nightly into restaurants, taverns, and theaters, including Ford's.

When Civil War broke out in April 1861, Washington lay open to attack from Virginia, just across the Potomac River, and from Confederate sympathizers in neighboring Maryland. To protect the city and vital supply routes, the Union Army built a ring of earthen fortifications around the outskirts of the capital. The remains of several are preserved today by the National Park Service as Fort Circle Parks.

"The scenery around Washington is really fine, the Potomac a lordly river... very fine, nothing petty about it—the Washington monument, not half finished—the public grounds around it filled with ten thousand beeves on the hoof— to the left the Smithsonian with its brown turrets—to the far right across, Arlington heights, the forts, eight or ten of them— then the long bridge, and down a ways but quite plain, the shipping of Alexandria."

Walt Whitman, March 19, 1863

President Lincoln considered the completion of the Capitol dome an important symbol of his commitment to unifying the country. Work continued unabated throughout the war, and the Statue of Freedom was placed atop the finished dome on December 2, 1863. After the assassination, Lincoln would lie in state in the recently completed Rotunda.

The Long Bridge connected Washington, D.C., to the Virginia shore at the current location of the 14th Street Bridge.

The Washington Monument remained unfinished throughout the Civil War. Grounds surrounding the monument were used as a stockyard for cattle to supply the troops. It was not completed until 1884.

Below: Union troops used the land between the Capitol and the Washington Monument as parade and training grounds.

The History of Ford's Theatre
1861-1863

Theater entrepreneur John T. Ford arrived in Washington, D.C., in 1861, looking for an opportunity, and he found it in the deserted First Baptist Church on Tenth Street, NW. On November 19, 1861, Ford opened his Washington career with an opera featuring Miss Carlotta Patti. In the following weeks, he staged several more productions to test the uncertain wartime entertainment market.

Ford was encouraged by the success of these musical productions, and he decided to invest in a larger venue to rival the famous Grover's National Theatre on Pennsylvania Avenue, also under construction at the time. When Ford leased the old church, one staunch parishioner predicted a dire fate for a house of worship transformed into a music hall. For the time being, however, luck was on Ford's side.

After three hectic days of remodeling, Ford reopened his new music hall on December 10, 1861. He rented the space to George Christy, who advertised as

Early playbills of Ford's Theatre advertised a variety of entertainment, from grand operas to spectacular military dramas.

"The George Christy Opera House." Ford's name did not appear on the advertisements for Christy's Minstrels, who headlined for two months.

According to playbills, general admission cost $1.00 and reserved seats an additional 50 cents. The two prices for admission indicate that no major structural changes had been made to the interior of the building, and that the basic seating arrangement of the church pews and balcony remained intact. Mr. W. G. Metzerott sold tickets for the performances from his music store on the corner of Eleventh Street and Pennsylvania Avenue, NW.

Washington's population soared from 60,000 to 200,000 during the war, and residents and wartime visitors alike flocked to the music hall. The city's population swelled with thousands of Northern soldiers who reported to the Capital throughout 1861, awaiting uniforms, arms, and military assignments. For entertainment, they, too, went to Ford's Theatre.

The theater was so successful that in February 1862, Ford committed an additional $10,000 to remodel the stage for theatrical as well as musical productions. James J. Gifford, the chief carpenter of the Ford's Holliday Street Theatre in Baltimore, drew up the plans. Joseph Parker painted allegorical murals of the four seasons, and of artists such as Shakespeare, Mozart, and Edwin Forrest, an enormously popular American actor. Just nineteen days later, "Ford's Atheneum" opened with Lucille Western starring in "The French Spy." The new playbills listed John T. Ford as both owner and manager. The programs also "trustfully solicit[ed] the indulgence of the patrons" during the ongoing construction in the unfinished theater.

As romantic visions of a three-month war faded with the disastrous Union retreat at Bull Run and the bloody victory at Shiloh in April 1862, Washingtonians sought diversion and entertainment in a frenzied array of activities. Party goers had four or five options every evening. There were dances at Willard's Hotel, plays at Ford's Theatre and Grover's National Theatre, and operas during the winter season. Hotels, saloons, and less-than-reputable dance halls catered to boisterous crowds every night. Sportsmen raced horses along E Street until a "trotting course" opened across the river, and baseball games attracted increasing crowds of spectators.

President Lincoln, known for his appreciation of the theater, first attended Ford's on May 28, 1862. His presence added prestige to an already distinguished list of patrons. Lincoln, who also attended Grover's Theatre often, worried that "some think I do wrong to go to the opera and theater, but it relieves my heavy burden" in the dark days of the war.

John T. Ford

John T. Ford, a fiery red-haired theater entrepreneur with the ambition to match, came from Baltimore to Washington in 1861 in search of a location for a new venue. Ford was well known in theater circles as an enterprising and energetic businessman. He managed the Holliday Street Theatre, or "Old Drury," as it was more commonly known, in Baltimore and the Academy of Music in Philadelphia. Baltimore's Holliday Street Theatre, built in 1796, was one of the oldest theaters in the United States. Throughout the course of his career, Ford would own successful playhouses in New York, Philadelphia, Baltimore, Washington, and Richmond, and establish himself as a central figure in nineteenth-century American theater.

James Ford

Brother of John Ford and business manager of Ford's Theatre, James was in charge of the theater on the evening of April 14, 1865, while John was away in Richmond. Another brother, Harry Ford, decorated the State Box when he was notified that President Lincoln and his guests would be attending the theater that evening.

The Emancipation Proclamation

Lincoln with his Cabinet (left to right): Secretary of War Edwin Stanton, Secretary of the Treasury Salmon Chase, Secretary of the Navy Gideon Welles, Attorney General James Speed, Secretary of State William Seward, Postmaster William Dennison, and Secretary of the Interior John Usher. The artist's rendering by Francis Bicknell Carpenter depicts the President holding his handwritten manuscript of the Proclamation (below.)

In the latter months of 1862, the tides of battle favored the Union armies with victories in the Mississippi Valley, and at Antietam and Murfreesboro. President Lincoln had been waiting anxiously for a Union victory to deliver his Emancipation Proclamation, freeing those enslaved throughout the states in rebellion as of January 1, 1863. He had his opportunity with the Confederate withdrawal at Antietam in September 1862.

Lincoln's proclamation partially followed and partially led a fundamental change in the purpose of the Civil War. Prior to the Emancipation

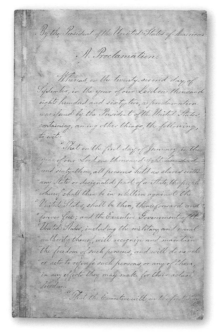

Proclamation, the official goal of the war was the preservation of the Union, with or without slavery. As the Union armies occupied slave-holding territory, however, thousands of those held in bondage ran to Union lines for protection as "contraband." Union and abolition of the "peculiar institution" of slavery gradually became one in the same end, creating a tidal wave of social change that can be appreciated only in hindsight.

Lincoln's proclamation was most revolutionary in that it put guns in the hands of thousands of African-American soldiers, inviting them to participate in the battle for their freedom. Public reaction in the North was mixed—some critics swearing they would never fight for the freedom of slaves, others complaining that the decree did too little by liberating slaves only where it could not be enforced. Southerners were predictably horrified by Lincoln's decree, envisioning massive slave uprisings and the wholesale murder of whites throughout the Confederacy.

In the Northern states and abroad, however, most rejoiced at the news of freedom. One-hundred-gun salutes were fired in cities and towns as newspapers published the Proclamation. Jubilant celebrations and prayer meetings were held throughout the night. In triumphant celebration of the Emancipation Proclamation, abolitionists Frederick Douglass, William Lloyd Garrison, Harriet Beecher Stowe, and hundreds more gathered in Boston's Music Hall on New Year's Eve to count down to the long-awaited freedom of enslaved African Americans.

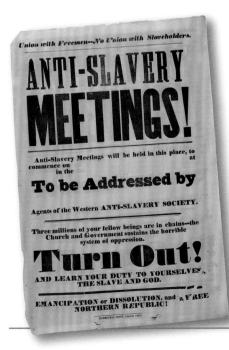

The American Abolitionist Movement

Slavery became an issue that split the nation. Abolitionist literature began to appear in 1820 and anti-slavery meetings were announced by handbills (below left) or by advertisements in local newspapers. The engraving (above) is from an American anti-slavery almanac for 1840 published in New York.

The first openly abolitionist literature began to appear around 1820, although opposition to slavery pre-dated the United States itself. In 1831, a radical abolitionist named William Lloyd Garrison began publishing *The Liberator*, an anti-slavery newspaper advocating the immediate emancipation of all slaves. Two years later, he helped form the American Anti-Slavery Society, which hosted speakers like former slave Frederick Douglass, who went on to become one of the most well known and respected abolitionist leaders of the nineteenth century. Author Harriet Beecher Stowe wrote her contro-versial novel *Uncle Tom's Cabin* in 1852, focusing national attention on the issue of slavery. When she met President Lincoln in the White House in 1862, legend claims that he welcomed her as "the little lady who made this big war."

Until the Civil War began in 1861, the anti-slavery press produced a steady stream of newspapers, periodicals, sermons, children's publications, speeches, abolitionist society reports, broadsides, and memoirs of former slaves. They pressured President Lincoln to free American slaves and fought for the civil rights of the freedmen after the Civil War.

Fire!

As Northerners celebrated hard-won military victories and abolitionists and slaves anticipated the jubilee, disaster struck at Ford's Theatre. Nine months after the theater's grand opening, at about 5 o'clock on the bitterly cold evening of December 30, 1862, a defective gas meter ignited a fire under the stage. One of the most spectacular fires in the Capital's history burned throughout the night. One local paper reported that the flames were so bright in the night sky "it was not difficult to read print in the open air at almost any point within the city limits."

By the next morning, the theater had been completely gutted; only the blackened interior walls remained standing among the charred rubble. Luckily, no one had been injured in the blaze, and most of the costume collection, sent to Baltimore the night before, was spared. Ford estimated his losses, only partially covered by fire insurance, at $20,000, an astounding sum at the time.

Financing a Greater Venture:
The New Ford's Theatre

Characteristically undiscouraged, Ford immediately resolved to build a grander, more modern theater on the charred site. Neighboring buildings on the north and south sides, which had also been damaged in the fire, were torn down to make room for the planned 2,500-seat structure. Ford purchased part of the lot to the north from Robert D. Clokey. He leased part of the south lot from William H. Phillips for the next ninety-nine years.

Despite wartime shortages in building materials and labor, several factors worked to Ford's advantage. The Northern wartime economy remained relatively stable in 1863. The previous year, Congress had passed two far-reaching fiscal policies to finance the costly war. In February, the National Banking Act created a national currency of "greenbacks." Although not backed by specie, the strength of Northern manufactures and public confidence inspired by recent military victories ensured its stability. Also in 1862, the government instituted the Bureau of Internal Revenue to collect the first federal income tax. Overall, these measures kept inflation in the Union to a difficult but manageable 80 percent throughout the war, compared to a crippling rate of 9000 percent in the Confederacy.

In order to raise the needed funds for construction of his new theater, Ford devised three strategies: loans on his property, the sale of stock certificates, and a congressional charter for the incorporation of the Washington Theatre Company. The sympathetic Washington community pitched in to help. Even Ford's main rival, the Grover's National Theatre, hosted a benefit performance to raise funds for new construction.

Favorable news coverage and his upstanding professional reputation gained Ford the financial backing of some of the most influential businessmen in Washington. With Ford, Richard Wallace, the mayor of Wash-

Proposed charter for financing the Washington Theatre Company.

ington; George W. Riggs, president of Riggs National Bank; James C. McGuire, Joseph F. Brown, A. R. Potts, Franklin Tenney, and Thomas Berry formed the Washington Theatre Company and petitioned Congress for incorporation. The bill narrowly passed in the House of Representatives, but stalled in the Senate. No action had been taken when the thirty-seventh Congress adjourned, and the bill died on the floor.

Despite the failure of the incorporation bill, Ford progressed with the construction of the new theater, determined to finance the venture through loans and the sale of stocks. His estimated cost of construction was $75,000, an enormous sum at the time, especially considering wartime scarcity and high labor costs. In April 1863, Ford began soliciting subscribers to purchase $500 shares of stock, payable with interest at any time during the next ten years. Shareholders were entitled to free admission to all performances at Ford's until the debt was paid. Among the names of the original shareholders were Maggie Mitchell, one of the leading comediennes of the time; John F. Coyle, editor of the *National Intelligencer*; and Henry Polkinhorn, printer of Ford's playbills. Since some of the stock certificates were re-dated August 1863, Ford probably sold additional stock to meet unforeseen construction costs.

Ford's New Theatre
1863-1865

The cornerstone of Ford's New Theatre was laid amid much fanfare on February 28, 1863. Architect James J. Gifford again designed and supervised the construction of the theater, but there were difficulties. The builders encountered problems with the structure's foundation.

Underlying quicksand and resulting cave-ins postponed work for almost three weeks before the foundation walls were finally built on a firm layer of blue clay. A shortage of bricks, although easily remedied by importing more from Baltimore, caused further delay. Work that was expected to last only seventy-five days dragged on until August.

Contemporary illustrations indicate that Gifford relied heavily on the plan of the Holliday Street Theatre in Baltimore, which he created in 1854, in designing Ford's new Washington theater. Gifford's original plans for Ford's included the five arched doors,

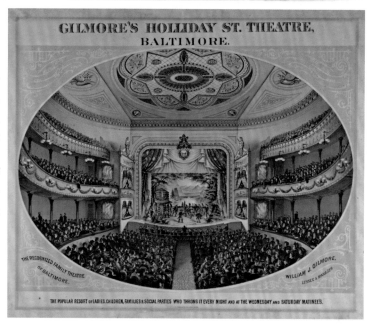

Both Ford's Theatre and the Holliday Street Theatre in Baltimore were owned by John T. Ford and designed by James J. Gifford. Gifford relied heavily on the plan of the Holliday Street Theatre when he created Ford's Theatre.

pilasters, elaborate cornice, and statues seen on the Baltimore theater. However, the cornice and pediment remained unfinished until late in 1865, and the statues were never added to Ford's Theatre.

To accommodate the increasing crowds in the Nation's Capital, Ford enlarged the theater with additional wings on both the north and south sides. There were new dressing rooms for the actors and a carpenter's shop. On the south side, a three-story brick addition housed a restaurant and bar, Peter Taltavul's Star Saloon, on the first floor. A double door on the second floor accessed the cloakroom and a lounge for the theater's dress circle, or first balcony level. James Ford and his brother, Harry Clay Ford, lived in an apartment on the third floor of the south wing, which they could reach from the second or third floors of the theater.

Enthusiastic newspaper descriptions notwithstanding, Ford's Theatre remained unfinished when it opened to the public in August 1863. Among other problems, the exterior brickwork was of poor quality, the wooden lookouts built to support the non-existent cornice and pediment were exposed, and the

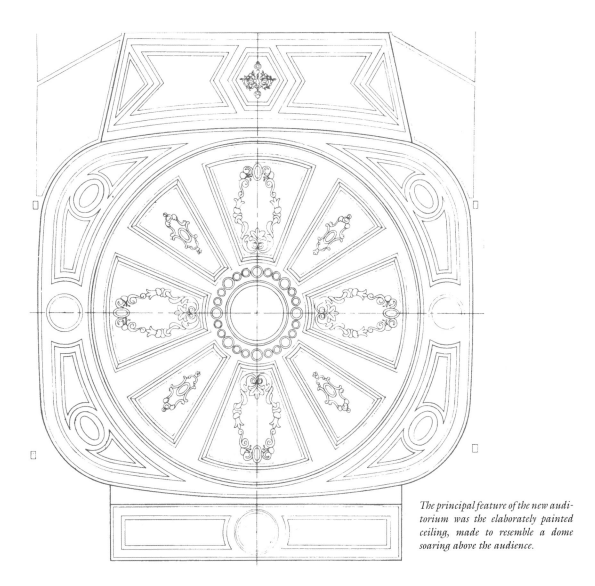

The principal feature of the new auditorium was the elaborately painted ceiling, made to resemble a dome soaring above the audience.

Tenth Street facade bulged noticeably outward.

Without a doubt, the lavish interior decor of the theater far outshone the incomplete exterior. Local journalists extolled the virtues of the building as it neared completion. The Washington *Sunday Chronicle* reported that the theater was "an ornament to the city" whose "elegance has few superiors." All the latest advances in the "science of acoustics" ensured that every member in the audience could hear even the lowest of stage whispers, and the scenery moved mechanically on tracks set in the stage. Modern methods of ventilation provided a constant supply of fresh air, and the addition of hoses and water pipes throughout protected against fire. Inside, patrons were "struck by the remarkable appearance of spaciousness and elegance" of the main hall.

The theater was divided into three seating levels. The gradually sloping ground level held approximately 600 movable wooden chairs with cane seats. The chairs were not attached to the floor so that the entire area could be made even with the stage for dances. There were half-circular niches on the aisles to the rear of the parquet, perhaps to accommodate heating stoves or busts of theater personalities. The second floor balcony, or dress circle, accommodated 420 people in wooden chairs similar to those on the level

Above left: These keys unlocked the doors to the State Box, where the Lincolns and their guests sat, enjoying the play. Above right: The restored State Box with the original loveseat from the evening of April 14, 1865.

below. Finally, the upper tier, or family circle balcony, seated 600 to 700 people on high wooden benches. Gas lighting fixtures ran the entire length of the ornate railing along this upper balcony, and on special occasions, birdcages hung from the fixtures. The spacious auditorium was painted white with gold trim, and ornamental plaster moldings adorned the walls and railings. The principal feature of the auditorium was an elaborately painted ceiling made to resemble a dome rising forty-nine feet above the audience.

Four private boxes, arranged in two tiers, flanked either side of the stage. The more elaborate and desirable upper boxes provided an excellent view of the stage and the audience. When the two upper boxes on stage left, boxes seven and eight, were combined, they were known collectively as the State Box, which was reserved for use by high government officials. This is also known as the Presidential Box.

The Grand Opening

The grand opening at Ford's Theatre coincided with the festive mood in Washington. The Capital City was still buzzing with the July 1863 Union victories at Gettysburg and Vicksburg. These triumphs destroyed Confederate hopes for European recognition and proved in retrospect to be the turning points of the Civil War. Buoyed by the recent military successes, Washingtonians turned out in large numbers for Ford's grand opening on Thursday evening, August 27, 1863. Ford's "New Theatre" opened with a sold-out performance of the dramatic romance, *The Naiad Queen.*

Ford's Theatre quickly returned to full operation, staging 495 performances during the 1863-65 seasons. Ford attracted a procession of great stars to Washington and boasted one of the best stock companies on the American stage.

John Wilkes Booth, a successful young star of the era, performed several times at Ford's Theatre. Though only in his twenties, Booth had enjoyed an early rise to prominence on the American stage, partially due to the fame of his father, the English tragedian Junius Brutus Booth.

The critics hailed Booth's dramatic talents on the stage, and his dark good looks made him one of the most popular matinee idols of his time. Booth was best known for his performances in Shakespearean dramas, and especially for his role as Marc Antony in *Julius Caesar.*

Another devoted fan of Shakespeare and the theater, President Lincoln attended at least a dozen shows at Ford's Theatre, including one where Booth had a leading role, *The Marble Heart,* on November 9, 1863, only ten days before the President delivered his memorable Gettysburg Address.

John Wilkes Booth

In early 1861, a popular young actor named John Wilkes Booth began his first tour of Northern theaters with a performance in Albany, New York. The dashing young actor, whom John Ford described as "the most handsome man I'd ever seen," had spent the previous two years traveling the theatrical circuit in the South, absorbing the growing secessionist fervor and enchanting his public. Despite his outspoken expression of Southern sympathies, Booth's talents on the stage made him a favorite with both Northern critics and audiences, and his dark flashing eyes and magnetic charm endeared him to the ladies. Booth's promising career persuaded him to stay in the North when the war broke out on April 14, 1861, with the Union surrender of Fort Sumter.

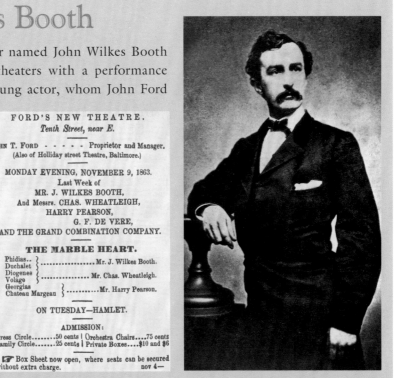

Playbill from the November 7, 1863, production of "The Marble Heart," at which Abraham Lincoln enjoyed John Wilkes Booth's performance at Ford's Theatre.

The Gettysburg Address

The Battle of Gettysburg marked Lee's final invasion of the North, and his defeat was a turning point in the war. For three days, July 1-3, 1863, the battle raged in the little Pennsylvania town where more than 51,000 men were killed or wounded in the fighting. President Lincoln was called upon to help dedicate a cemetery to those fallen soldiers. On November 19, 1863, Lincoln delivered perhaps his best-known speech and one of the finest examples of American oratory.

Parade of Union troops entering Gettysburg, Pennsylvania, before President Lincoln gave his famous Gettysburg Address on November 19, 1863.

"*FOUR SCORE AND SEVEN YEARS AGO our fathers brought forth, upon this continent, a new nation, conceived in Liberty, and dedicated to the proposition that all men are created equal.*

Now we are engaged in a great civil war, testing whether that nation, or any nation so conceived, and so dedicated, can long endure. We are met here on a great battlefield of that war. We have come to dedicate a portion of it as a final resting place for those who here gave their lives that that nation might live. It is altogether fitting and proper that we should do this.

But in a larger sense we can not dedicate — we can not consecrate — we can not hallow this ground. The brave men, living and dead, who struggled here, have consecrated it far above our poor power to add or detract. The world will little note, nor long remember, what we say here, but can never forget what they did here. It is for us, the living, rather to be dedicated here to the unfinished work which they have, thus far, so nobly carried on. It is rather for us to be here dedicated to the great task remaining before us — that from these honored dead we take increased devotion to that cause for which they here gave the last full measure of devotion — that we here highly resolve that these dead shall not have died in vain; that this nation shall have a new birth of freedom; and that this government of the people, by the people, for the people, shall not perish from the earth."

A Lincoln

A Country Divided

Artist James Hope, a forty-three-year-old soldier of the Second Vermont Infantry, sketched and later painted Union General Burnside's attack over the bridge at Antietam on September 17, 1862. Almost 23,000 soldiers were killed or wounded during the Battle of Antietam.

The issues of slavery and states rights divided a nation and tested the fundamental principles of the young country. Representing this ambivalence were the four crucial border states that hung in the balance throughout the war, refusing to join the Confederacy, yet denying support to the Union. A slave state before the war, Maryland was home to a large secessionist minority. Riots and attacks on Union troops traveling through the state prompted President Lincoln to invoke his questionable Constitutional powers to keep Maryland in the Union by force of martial law.

President Lincoln's war measures infuriated Confederates, as well as some loyal Unionists. Following the Union surrender of Fort Sumter near Charleston, South Carolina, at the beginning of the war, the President called for 75,000 troops and ordered a blockade of Confederate ports without consulting Congress. Then Lincoln spent two million dollars of public funds from the national treasury to equip this army, again without the consent of Congress.

In one of his most controversial policies, Lincoln suspended the writ of habeas corpus, giving himself the right to arrest and, without trial or charge, imprison individuals who "endangered the public safety." Using this power, he had thirty-one seces-

sionist members of the Maryland state legislature arrested the night before that assembly planned to vote Maryland out of the Union. Outspoken journalists and other Maryland protesters who denounced Lincoln's actions shortly followed the legislators to prison.

Lincoln felt these drastic moves necessary to keep Maryland from following neighboring Virginia to the Confederacy. If Maryland were to secede, Washington, D.C., would be surrounded by enemy territory, a situation Lincoln was determined to avoid.

The President replied to Supreme Court Justice Roger B. Taney's stern admonition regarding the long-standing tradition of habeas corpus with a practical response. During the extraordinary time of war, Lincoln asserted, it was his sworn duty to administer the laws and protect the public safety by taking extraordinary measures, if necessary. "Are all the laws but one to go unexecuted," he asked, "and the government itself go to pieces, lest that one be violated?" His critics, however, accused the President of abusing the Constitution and denying the civil liberties of citizens. Cries of "tyrant" and "dictator" echoed throughout the critical press.

As expressed in both his first and his second inaugural addresses, and in many recorded statements and personal letters, Lincoln firmly believed his primary duty was to preserve the Union and to administer its laws faithfully, as he had sworn to do when administered the oath of office. In his first inaugural address, he asserted that "in view of the Constitution and the laws, the Union is unbroken." He assured Southerners that "the property, peace and security of no section are to be endangered by the incoming Administration." The very idea of secession, according to Lincoln, was "the essence of anarchy." The Founding Fathers had taken every precaution to ensure that the Union was perpetual, as was implied in the Constitution, and he meant to uphold this conviction.

In an August 1862 letter to Horace Greeley, Lincoln wrote: "If there be those who would not save the Union, unless they could at the same time save slavery, I do not agree with them. If there be those who would not save the Union unless they could at the same time destroy slavery, I do not agree with them. My paramount object in this struggle is to save the Union, and is not either to save or to destroy slavery. If I could save the Union without freeing any slave I would do it, and if I could save it by freeing all the slaves I would do it; and if I could save it by freeing some and leaving others alone I would also do that. What I do about slavery, and the colored race, I do because I believe it helps to save the Union; and what I forbear, I forbear because I do not believe it would help to save the Union."

Lincoln had been elected to guide the nation, and he meant to see that when he left office, it was as the President of the entire United States of America. It was to this end that Lincoln approached decisions and interpreted the laws of the land. The perpetuation of the Union and of popular government came before all other considerations.

Horace Greeley

Horace Greeley was the founding editor of the New York *Tribune*, one of the first American "penny daily" newspapers. An outspoken and eccentric editor, Greeley was an influential political force throughout the 1850s and 1860s. Using his paper as a platform, Greeley advocated westward expansion and a transcontinental railroad, temperance, organized labor, and the immediate abolition of slavery. Always prone to sudden shifts of opinion, he vacillated unpredictably between pacifism and calls of "On to Richmond!" throughout the Civil War. President Lincoln often acknowledged Greeley's influence on public opinion and responded several times to critical editorials in the *Tribune*. After the South's surrender in 1865, Greeley posted bail for former Confederate President Jefferson Davis, a highly unpopular act that cost the *Tribune* thousands of readers. In 1872, Greeley was nominated as the Democratic candidate for President but lost by a landslide to incumbent President Ulysses S. Grant. Greeley died one month later.

The Border States

Lying roughly along a line from the Potomac River to the Nebraska frontier, the four border states of Delaware, Maryland, Kentucky, and Missouri were contested territory for both the Union and the Confederacy, each needing their support and resources to win the war. All four were slave states with pro-secessionist minorities of varying strength. Delaware was the most loyal to the Union; Maryland the least. Federal troops remained in eastern Maryland for the duration of the war to control secessionist activity and protect Washington, D.C. Kentucky and Missouri attempted to remain neutral, but eventually federal troops occupied these states as well. Ultimately, all four border states remained in the Union, but thousands of their citizens chose to fight for the Confederacy, making the Civil War a tragic fight of brother against brother, neighbor against neighbor.

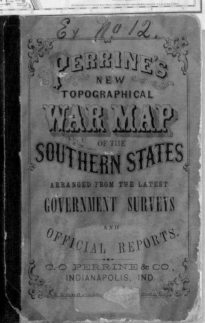

When John Wilkes Booth was captured, after Lincoln's assassination, this "War Map of the Southern States" was found in his possession.

Ulysses S. Grant

Born on April 22, 1822, Grant was the son of an Ohio tanner. He attended West Point without much enthusiasm and graduated in the middle of his class. Early in his military career, he fought under General Zachary Taylor in the Mexican War (1846-48). At the outbreak of the Civil War, Grant was working in his father's leather store in Galena, Illinois. He was appointed commander of a local volunteer regiment, and gradually rose through the ranks of the Union army. In the Mississippi Valley campaign, Grant took Fort Henry and would accept nothing less than "unconditional surrender" at Fort Donelson, earning himself a new nickname.

President Lincoln defended Grant's heavy losses at Shiloh in April 1862, saying, "I can't spare this man—he fights." After his stunning successes in the western theater at Vicksburg, in July 1863, Lincoln appointed him general-in-chief in March 1864. General Grant personally accepted the Confederate surrender at Appomattox Court House on April 9, 1865.

Grant's military reputation would later win for him two terms in the White House, from 1869 to 1877. In 1884, Grant became a partner in a financial firm, which eventually went bankrupt. Shortly after, he learned that he was dying of throat cancer, perhaps from smoking from seven to ten cigars per day. The ailing general began writing his memoirs to pay off his debts and provide for his family. Soon after completing the book in 1885, he died at age sixty-three.

The Union and Confederate battle flags. There were several Confederate flags used throughout the war. This flag (at right) was more commonly flown than the familiar "Stars and Bars."

Robert E. Lee

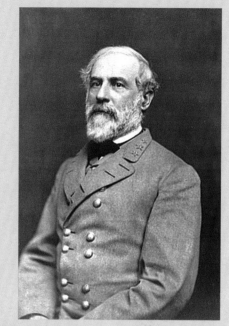

Robert E. Lee was born on January 19, 1807, at Stratford, Virginia, the fourth child of Revolutionary War hero "Lighthorse Harry" Lee and Ann Hill Carter Lee. As a young man, he was accepted to the U. S. military academy at West Point and graduated second in his class. In 1832, he married Mary Custis, the granddaughter of George and Martha Custis Washington, at their Arlington, Virginia, plantation on a hill overlooking Washington, D.C. Lee served honorably in the Mexican War and later as an army engineer. He divided his time between the family home at Arlington, located in what is now Arlington National Cemetery, and his military post.

In 1859, Lee helped put down John Brown's attempted rebellion at Harpers Ferry, Virginia. When his beloved state of Virginia followed South Carolina out of the Union after Lincoln's election, Lee made an agonizing decision. He turned down General Winfield Scott's offer to take command of the U. S. army and resigned his commission, leaving shortly thereafter for Richmond, where he would eventually accept command of the Confederate forces.

After four long years of war, General Lee surrendered at Appomattox Court House on April 9, 1865, effectively bringing the American Civil War to an end. Following the war, Lee urged his fellow Confederates to "Abandon your animosities and make your sons Americans." In 1865, he was offered the post of president of Washington College (now Washington and Lee University) in Lexington, Virginia, where he served until his death on October 12, 1870.

The Plot Thickens

Completed in early 1864, Andersonville prison was intended to house no more than 10,000 soldiers. By August, the population swelled to more than 33,000 Union prisoners of war. The painting done from memory by Thomas O'Dea shows the overcrowded conditions. Lack of food and poor sanitation killed more than 13,000 prisoners in the fourteen months of the prison's existence.

Although early in the war he considered himself a Unionist, John Wilkes Booth was infuriated by what he considered Lincoln's blatant suppression of basic political rights and the horrific threat of freeing nearly four million enslaved African Americans in the South. Throughout the early years of the war, Booth privately fumed over the President's policies, and secretly rebelled by serving as a Confederate agent. His subversive work brought him into contact with other members of the Confederate underground who would eventually assist in his plot to kidnap the President.

As the war progressed and its goal changed from one of union to one of freedom, Booth became more convinced of the necessity for action. Booth devoted more time and attention to his subversive activities. He ended his full-time

African-American soldiers were armed after the issuance of the Emancipation Proclamation on January 1, 1863. Approximately 180,000 African Americans served in the Union army during the Civil War.

theatrical career with a Boston performance in late May 1864.

Throughout the summer of 1864, the Northern press seethed with debates over General Grant's advice to the Lincoln administration to suspend all prisoner exchanges. From July 1862 until May 1863, there was an official exchange policy that called for captured soldiers of equal rank to be traded on a one-for-one basis, four privates for one lieutenant, and sixty privates for a general. When the Union army began to employ African-American troops, the Confederate government declared that all captured African-American soldiers, fugitive or free, would be enslaved. Until these soldiers were acknowledged as legitimate prisoners of war, the North suspended all exchanges. Prisons swelled with men who quickly fell victim to malnutrition and disease.

Grant was tough, and—unlike many of Lincoln's earlier military commanders—willing to act. He had earned the nickname "Unconditional Surrender" Grant for his refusal to accept anything less from the Confederate forces at Fort Donelson. Grant and his supporters reasoned that the greater population of the North would eventually win a grisly contest of numbers, because the Confederacy desperately needed their soldiers returned to continue the war effort. Adding to the furor, in August, the Union army issued the so-called "Retalia-

tion Order" that cut prisoner-of-war rations to a level believed equal to those issued to Union prisoners in Southern camps. In effect, this order meant thousands would starve, and it sparked a flurry of activity in the Confederate underground movement, as prisoner exchange became critical to the survival of the Confederacy.

Plans to capture presidents Lincoln and Davis, the Confederate leader, were fairly common as schemes to induce large-scale prisoner exchanges. Most schemes were considered well within the rules of warfare. The Confederate government, according to some scholars, initiated at least two such plans to abduct President Lincoln. One unproven plot would be revealed during the trial of Booth's con-

spirators. Conspirator George Atzerodt made a statement at his 1865 trial in which he told of Booth's knowledge of a Confederate plot to blow up the White House. As for Union plots against the Confederate leader, in March 1864, unsigned orders were found on the corpse of a Union soldier commanding him to burn Richmond and kill President Jefferson Davis.

Booth devised his own plan to re-institute prisoner exchange policies: he would capture President Lincoln and transport him through sympathetic country in southern Maryland to Richmond, Virginia. Lincoln would be held hostage in the Confederate capital until he could be exchanged for thousands of Confederate prisoners of war.

Poor sanitation was a major cause of disease and death among prisoners of war in both the North and South. Above, captured Confederate soldiers at Fort Delaware, in Delaware City, Delaware.

Booth's Supporting Actors

Throughout the fall and winter of 1864, Booth recruited old friends and former schoolmates from Baltimore, Samuel Arnold and Michael O'Laughlin, both Confederate veterans, to participate in his plan. Booth invited several others into the conspiracy to capture President Lincoln: Lewis T. Powell, a Confederate deserter; German immi-

Samuel Arnold

George Andrew Atzerodt

David Herold

Samuel Arnold was born in the Georgetown neighborhood of Washington, D.C., on September 6, 1834. Later, his family moved to Baltimore, and Samuel attended St. Timothy's Hall, a military academy, with John Wilkes Booth. Arnold joined the Confederate army during the Civil War but was discharged for health reasons. He returned to Baltimore, and in the late summer of 1864, was recruited by Booth to be part of the plot to capture President Lincoln. Arnold was arrested on April 17, 1865. He admitted his part in the plot to capture Lincoln. Although his co-workers supported Arnold's contention that he was in Virginia at the time of the assassination, the U.S. Government charged him with conspiracy, and he went to trial. Arnold was found guilty by the military commission and sentenced to life in prison in Ft. Jefferson in the Dry Tortugas.

George Andrew Atzerodt was born in 1835 in Thuringen, Germany. At the age of eight, he came to America and settled in Maryland. Before the Civil War, Atzerodt settled in Port Tobacco, Maryland, with his older brother, John, where they set up a carriage repair shop. During the Civil War, George began rowing Confederate friends back and forth across the Potomac River, and became acquainted with a Confederate messenger named John Surratt. In the assassination plot that unfolded after the kidnapping attempt failed, Atzerodt was assigned to kill Vice President Andrew Johnson. Whether Atzerodt ever agreed to do this remains unknown, but he made no attempt on the life of Andrew Johnson. He was hanged on July 7, 1865.

David Herold was born June 16, 1842, in Washington, D.C. He was the sixth of eleven children born to a financially secure couple, Adam and Mary Porter Herold. As a child, David liked to go bird hunting and spent several months every year roaming the Maryland countryside. He attended Rittenhouse Academy and studied pharmacy at Georgetown College. He later worked for several druggists in Washington. Herold met Booth either through his friendship with Surratt or in 1863, when Booth purchased medicine to treat a growth on his neck. Herold may have provided the drugs that Booth smuggled to the South. Herold was found guilty of conspiracy and sentenced to hang. His mother and many of his eight sisters visited him while he awaited execution. Herold was hanged on July 7, 1865. He had no last words.

The conspirators were imprisoned in the Washington Penitentiary under heavy guard. All but Mary Surratt and Dr. Mudd wore heavy canvas hoods, shackles, and handcuffs.

grant George Atzerodt, who supplied a boat meant to ferry the captured President across the Potomac River and south toward Richmond; and young David Herold, a pharmacy clerk who supplied much-needed medicines to the Confederacy. While exploring possible escape routes through southern Maryland, where they could rely on Confederate supporters for assistance, Booth met Dr. Samuel A. Mudd of Bryantown, another Confederate sympathizer. Dr. Mudd introduced John Wilkes Booth to John Surratt, a Confederate blockade runner, in Washington on December 23, 1864, and Surratt willingly joined in the conspiracy to capture the President.

Lewis Thornton Powell

Michael O'Laughlin

Mary Elizabeth Surratt

Lewis Thornton Powell (also known as Lewis Paine or Payne) was born April 22, 1844, in Randolph Co., Alabama. Powell had eight brothers and sisters, and his father was a Baptist preacher. Powell enlisted as a private in the Confederate army on May 30, 1861, shortly after the war broke out. He fought in the Battle of Gettysburg, where he was shot in the right wrist and taken prisoner. Later he was transferred to the West Buildings Hospital in Baltimore, from which he escaped and enlisted in Mosby's Virginia cavalry in the fall of 1863. Eventually, Powell left the cavalry and took the Oath of Allegiance to the Union on January 13, 1865. Powell probably met John Wilkes Booth through John Surratt. Tall and powerfully built, Powell was an ideal conspirator in the plan to capture Abraham Lincoln. In the later assassination plot, Powell was assigned to kill Secretary of State William Seward. For his attempt, he was hanged on July 7, 1865.

Michael O'Laughlin was born in Baltimore, Maryland, around 1838. He was one of John Wilkes Booth's earliest friends, as the Booth family lived across the street from the O'Laughlins. He made his living manufacturing ornamental plaster work and engravings. At the outbreak of the Civil War, O'Laughlin enlisted in the Confederate army but was discharged in June 1862. He returned to Baltimore and joined his brother in the feed and produce business. In the fall of 1864, O'Laughlin agreed to become a conspirator in the plot to kidnap Abraham Lincoln. After the failed capture plot, O'Laughlin left Washington and did not return until the day of the assassination. He was sentenced to life in prison for his involvement in the conspiracy. He died of yellow fever at Fort Jefferson in September 1867.

Mary Elizabeth Jenkins was born in June 1823 near Waterloo, Maryland. In 1840 she married John H. Surratt. The couple moved to his family's farm, and had three children. In 1851, fire destroyed the Surratt home. They then bought a new farm in what is now Clinton, Maryland, and by 1853 the family was living in a newly-constructed Surratt House and Tavern. On December 6, 1853, for $4,000, John Surratt bought the Washington, D.C., property that would later become Mary's ill-fated boardinghouse. Two years after her husband died, in October 1864, Mary and her daughter Anna moved to Washington, D.C., and rented the Surrattsville tavern to a man named John M. Lloyd. To make money, Mary rented rooms in her northwest Washington, D.C., residence, located at 541 (now 604) H Street. For her involvement in the conspiracy, Mary Surratt was hanged on July 7, 1865. She was the first woman executed by the U.S. Government.

John Wilkes Booth: A Modern Day Brutus?

Although his grandfather had helped runaway slaves escape to the North and his brother Edwin had voted for and supported Lincoln, Booth did not share his family's Union sympathies. He had grown up in Baltimore and considered himself a proud Southern patriot. What he saw as Lincoln's heavy-handed tactics in Maryland, his home state, further angered Booth. However, when the Civil War broke out, he did not enlist in the Confederate army in deference to his mother's fears for his safety. Instead, Booth continued to perform on Northern stages while using his wealth, fame, and consequent freedom of travel to smuggle medicine and supplies to the Confederacy.

Booth's acting career strongly influenced his political beliefs. He derived many of his ideas from his characters and experiences on the stage, especially from his role as Marc Antony in Shakespeare's *Julius Caesar*. In Booth's mind, slaying a diabolical tyrant was an honorable act, no more an unjustified murder than killing opposing soldiers on the battlefield. John Ford would later say that he believed that the public had made assassination almost respectable by applauding the theatrical heroes who killed in the name of liberty. America had a proud tradition, beginning with the American Revolution against Great Britain, of deposing autocrats

Shown left to right: John Wilkes Booth performing Julius Caesar *with his brothers Edwin Booth, considered the most famous Shakespearean actor of the 19th century, and Junius Booth, Jr.*

when they used their power. Booth felt that he was playing a vital role in the theater of war that surrounded him. As he fled south after the assassination, he wrote in the datebook he used to record his thoughts, "our

country owed all her troubles to him [Lincoln], and God simply made me the instrument of his punishment."

Booth was not insane when he killed President Lincoln; just one of the President's many critics, remarkable only for the extremity of his actions. According to assassination expert William Hanchett, "When Lincoln is seen as a leader dealing with controversial problems in tumultuous times, it is easier to understand why he was assassinated than when he is envisioned as a godlike figure hovering serenely above the storm. Only a madman would kill a god. Booth was not a madman; he believed he had good reason to take Lincoln's life. He was not alone."

During four years of war, thousands of Southern men would die on the battlefield for beliefs similar to Booth's. With death a commonplace occurrence, assassination seemed a logical response for John Wilkes Booth.

The Historical Julius Caesar

Julius Caesar had become the virtual dictator of the Roman Empire by 44 B.C., wielding power of such magnitude that several men of his own government planned to assassinate him. The plotters convinced Brutus, a very influential Roman, to join their conspiracy. Though a moralist and an idealist, Brutus believed that the only way to end Caesar's tyranny was to kill him.

"Fierce fiery warriors fought upon the clouds,
In ranks and squadrons and right form of war,
Which drizzled blood upon the Capitol."

— From William Shakespeare's *Julius Caesar*, Scene 2

The Capture Plot

By spring 1865, the conspirators had developed a plan and mapped out an escape route. They were ready to act. Booth decided to seize Lincoln on March 17 during one of the President's frequent and unguarded carriage rides. Lincoln often escaped from the city to a country house near the Soldiers' Home, two or three miles from the city. He traveled on horseback down isolated country roads, morning and night, alone and vulnerable to attack. In 1864, during one such ride, Lincoln narrowly escaped death as a gunshot zipped by his head, knocking his stovepipe hat to the ground. It is not known if this particular incident was an assassination attempt.

On the day of Booth's planned seizure, however, Lincoln made a last-minute schedule change, and his would-be captors waited in vain for his arrival. Ironically, Lincoln had gone instead to the National Hotel, where Booth was living at the time, to receive a captured Confederate battle flag from an Indiana regiment. After this failed capture attempt, Arnold, Surratt, and O'Laughlin abandoned the plot and left town for fear they had been discovered. Booth, however, waited in the wings for his next opportunity.

President Lincoln often escaped the oppressive heat of Washington summers at Anderson Cottage at the Soldiers' Home, a few miles north of the city. He also visited injured soldiers recovering from their wounds there.

> *"If I shall live,
> I shall remain
> President."*

A. Lincoln, October 19, 1864

Lincoln's second inauguration was followed by a reception at the White House that evening. The 1865 print (above) pictures the President greeting Mrs. Julia Grant, wife of General Ulysses S. Grant, as Vice President Andrew Johnson and Mrs. Lincoln look on.

Lincoln's Second Inaugural

The morning of March 4, 1865, President Lincoln's second inauguration, began dark and rainy. But a few moments before President Lincoln was sworn in, the mist and clouds cleared, and the sun shone brightly on the gathered crowd at the U.S. Capitol. Among the thousands was John Wilkes Booth, attending as the guest of his fiancée, Lucy Hale, the daughter of John P. Hale, the former U.S. Senator from New Hampshire. Photographer Alexander Gardner captured Booth standing directly above President Lincoln as he urged his fellow citizens, "With malice toward none; with charity for all...let us strive...to bind up the nation's wounds; to care for him who shall have borne the battle, and for his widow, and his orphan—to do all which may achieve and cherish a just, and a lasting peace...." Booth later confided to his actor friend Samuel Knapp Chester, "What an excellent chance I had to kill the President, if I had wished, on inauguration day!"

Photographer Alexander Gardner captured Lincoln's second inauguration. Below, Lincoln addresses the crowd from the U. S. Capitol building. The close-up at left reveals a man thought to be John Wilkes Booth standing above and to the right of the President. He is the figure wearing a top hat and standing next to the pillar. The image of Lincoln was blurred by a fingerprint.

The Fall of the Confederacy

Any one of thousands of Southerners could have fulfilled Booth's wish just a few weeks later. General Grant had broken through the defenses around Petersburg and Richmond, Virginia, on April 2, 1865, sending the Confederate government and military fleeing south. On the steamy spring morning of April 4, President Lincoln and his son Tad stepped off a barge onto the muddy banks of the James River in Richmond, the recently evacuated Confederate capital city. A jubilant crowd of African Americans immediately surrounded him, clasping his hand and blessing him, as tears of thanks poured down their faces. The President shook their hands, as tears welled up in his own eyes.

With an escort of only twelve men, Lincoln and Tad trudged two miles up the silent and dusty streets as thousands peered out their windows and doors, crowding one another to get a view of the man whose election had sparked four years of civil war. Now they saw a father with his son plodding among the ruins of their city, not victoriously, but with evident sadness at the destruction surrounding him. Not one soldier or citizen came to greet him; no one said a word.

Lincoln saw the desolation of

Left and inset: President Lincoln and his son Tad visited the captured Confederate capital city, Richmond, in April 1865. African Americans greeted the President with enthusiasm, while thousands of white residents of the city peered silently from their windows.

war and the pride of the South in the wreckage of still smoking, burned-out buildings, destroyed as the retreating army left the ashes of the city to its Union victors. When one of his guards recommended tearing down old Libby Prison, where thousands of Union prisoners of war had died, Lincoln said no, "Let it stand as a monument." Finally, the little cortege came to the deserted Confederate Congress building and Jefferson Davis's presidential mansion, where Lincoln, exhausted and sweaty, dropped heavily into the Confederate president's chair and wondered aloud if he might have a glass of water.

Jefferson Davis

Jefferson Davis was born on June 3, 1808, in Todd County, Kentucky, not far from where Abraham Lincoln was born eight months later. Unlike Lincoln, however, Davis was well educated, attending Transylvania University and West Point Military Academy. Poor health forced him to retire from the army in 1835, so he entered politics. Over the next twenty-six years, Davis served sixteen years in the U.S. Congress, resigning his Senate seat when Mississippi seceded from the Union in January 1861. "The people of the States now confederated," Davis said, "believe that to remain longer in the Union would subject them to con-tinuance of a disparaging discrimination, submission to which would be inconsistent with their welfare, and intolerable to a proud people. They therefore determine to sever its bounds and establish a new Confederacy for themselves."

For the next four years, Davis served as the president of the Confederate States of America. After the Confederacy lost the war, Davis was imprisoned in Fort Monroe, Virginia, for two years and indicted for treason. A group of influential Northerners signed a $100,000 bond for his freedom in 1867. Davis attempted several unsuccessful business ventures before his death in 1889.

"Something Decisive and Great Must Be Done"

Before Booth and his accomplices could organize a second capture attempt, fate intervened. On April 9, 1865, General Robert E. Lee honorably surrendered the tattered remnants of the Confederate Army of Northern Virginia to Union General Ulysses S. Grant at Appomattox Court House, Virginia. Although the soldiers were anxious to fight to the finish for their beloved general, Lee saw that further loss was pointless. "With an unceasing admiration of your constancy and devotion to your Country, and a grateful remembrance of your kind and generous consideration," General Lee bid his courageous men an affectionate farewell and sent them home to their families.

But the war was not over for John Wilkes Booth. Realizing that a captive Lincoln was useless to the Confederate cause, Booth decided "Because our cause, being almost lost, something decisive and great must be done."

For the rest of the nation, however, the decisive event, the Civil War, had finally come to an end. The bloodshed and terrible loss of the hostilities were over, and throughout the North, the war-weary were in the mood to celebrate. For the moment, the monumental tasks of healing the nation's wounds and rebuilding a peaceful union without slavery could wait. Parades, fetes, bonfires, illuminations, and speeches were the order of the day in the Nation's Capital. Revelers and music filled the streets throughout Northern cities; lights burned in saloons and homes long into the night and partygoers watched the glorious sun rise over a nation at peace the next morning.

An exultant crowd congregated in front of the White House on April 11, 1865, calling for speeches from President and Commander-in-Chief Lincoln, the hero of the day. John Wilkes Booth stood sullenly among his victorious enemies and listened as President Lincoln spoke about the complicated issues of Reconstruction. Lincoln recommended welcoming those Confederate states that passed a free state constitution, enfranchising the freedmen and offering to them all the benefits of citizenship. Infuriated, Booth fumed to his companion Lewis Powell, "That is the last speech he'll ever make. I'll run him through."

An even more determined Booth and the remaining conspirators met on the night of Thursday, April 13 to discuss a new plan: a most elaborate assassination plot.

Booth's conspiracy called for the simultaneous murders of Secretary of State William H. Seward, Vice President Andrew Johnson, and President Lincoln. According to a complicated law of succession adopted by Congress in 1792, the president of the Senate pro tempore, Senator Lafayette Foster from Connecticut, would act as temporary president if both the presidency and vice presidency were vacated. The law also directed the secretary of state to notify the state governors to assemble the Electoral College and elect a new president and vice president. In effect, killing the president, vice president, and secretary of state at once would throw the government into complete anarchy, perhaps allowing the Confederacy a longer life and second chance at victory.

Booth instructed Lewis Powell to kill Secretary of State William Seward and George Atzerodt to murder Vice President Andrew Johnson, while at the same appointed time, Booth himself would assassinate President Lincoln.

Confederate Involvement in the Lincoln Assassination

Almost immediately after Lincoln's death, rumors circulated that the Confederate government and the Copperheads—Northerners who opposed the war—were responsible for the assassination. Coded letters found in Booth's room at the National Hotel linked him to the Confederacy, and several witnesses came forward to offer evidence of Booth's meetings with Confederate agents in Canada in 1864.

A cipher machine capable of writing encoded secret messages was found in Jefferson Davis's office after the evacuation of Richmond. Although conclusive evidence never implicated Jefferson Davis in the assassination plot, belief in Confederate involvement has surged since the late 1970s, when an interesting piece of evidence resurfaced. During his trial, conspirator George Atzerodt told police that an attempt to blow up the White House in early April 1865 had failed. The transcript of this statement was discovered in 1977, and it supports the theory that the Lincoln assassination was part of a larger Confederate survival strategy.

Public sentiment for peace was strong in 1864, one of the most cru-

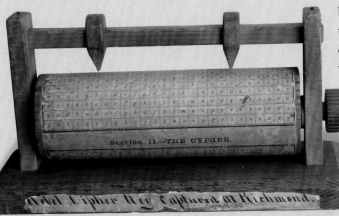

This cipher machine was captured in Richmond. Some view it as evidence of Confederate involvement in Lincoln's assassination since a code block was found in Booth's rented room.

cial election years in American history. If Lincoln had lost his bid for reelection, his Democratic successor may have ended the war, allowing the Southern states to depart from the Union with the institution of slavery intact. The Confederate government worked hard to prevent Lincoln's reelection, bankrolling Democratic candidates, buying off newspapers in the West, and publicizing Confederate peace offers that Lincoln refused to accept.

In October 1864, just prior to the election, Booth met with well-known Confederate politician George Sanders in Montreal, and it is known that Booth had been to Canada, a Confederate haven for spies, several times during the latter years of the war.

As the war situation became more desperate for the Confederacy, more daring and reckless plans were necessary to survive. In late November 1864, a small expedition of men left Canada for New York City, intending to burn the city to the ground. Others planned to invade Northern prisoner-of-war camps to free Southern soldiers whom Lincoln refused to exchange. In February 1865, the Confederate Congress created a Secret Service, whose duties included "the encouragement or application of new warlike inventions." Offers to capture or kill Lincoln poured into Jefferson Davis's office from both civilians and military personnel. It is unknown if Davis ever approved any of these schemes.

Historians have not found direct evidence of specific Confederate encouragement of Booth to kill President Lincoln. However, it seems likely that Booth came up with the idea to murder Lincoln, Johnson, and Seward in his meetings and dealings with Confederate agents.

Lincoln's Last Day

The next day, Good Friday, April 14, 1865, dawned gray and chilly. Yet neither this solemn Christian holiday nor the inclement weather could dampen the continuing revelry in the Capital City. Exactly four years to the day after Confederate rebels had hauled it down, the shell-torn Stars and Stripes was raised again over Fort Sumter at Charleston, South Carolina, the first battlesite of the war.

President Lincoln arose late for him, and went downstairs for his usual sparse breakfast of black coffee and one egg at around 7 a.m. According to Mrs. Lincoln, her husband was unusually cheerful that morning; after all, the long war was virtually over and his family was together again. Over breakfast, the Lincolns' oldest son Robert, a captain on General Grant's staff who had witnessed the recent surrender at Appomattox Court House, gave his father first-hand details of the event.

After breakfast, Lincoln met with his Cabinet from 11 a.m. until 1:30 p.m. to discuss the peaceful restoration of the Confederacy to the United States. Lincoln intended no more violence or retribution toward Southerners as they returned to the Union. General Grant attended the meeting to report on Lee's surrender at Appomattox.

While Lincoln worked at the White House, John Wilkes Booth unwittingly set out on his last day as a free man. As he left his room at the National Hotel early on the morning of April 14, Booth urged the hotel desk clerk to attend Ford's Theatre that evening, promising "some fine acting." Not realizing the full impact of his statement, Booth himself headed to the theater,

Victorious Union soldiers pose outside the McLean home in the village of Appomattox Court House, where Lee surrendered to Grant on April 9, 1865.

where he reportedly spent most of his free time. He had his mail delivered there, a common practice of the day among actors, and most of his friends, including owner John Ford and the other actors, usually congregated backstage or at the Star Saloon next door. Not surprisingly, Booth was sitting on the front steps

of the theater reading a letter when Mrs. Lincoln's messenger arrived at 10:30 a.m. to reserve the State Box for the Presidential party that night. Seizing his long-anticipated opportunity, Booth set his murderous plan in motion.

Days later, witnesses would testify that they saw Booth coming and going from Ford's throughout the afternoon, perhaps exploring an escape route from the building. Sometime after the morning rehearsal, Booth left a pine strut from a broken music stand in the hallway near the State Box, to be used later as a door brace. At around 2 p.m., Booth visited the Herndon House, where he instructed fellow conspirator Lewis Powell to assassinate Secretary of State William Seward that very night. Then Booth went in search of George Atzerodt to inform him of his role in the plot: to kill Vice President Andrew Johnson. Each conspirator was to commit the act at 10:15 p.m., then meet at the Navy Yard Bridge to escape south through Maryland. At about 2:30, Booth visited Mary Surratt's boardinghouse and asked her to deliver a package containing a pair of field glasses to her tavern in Surrattsville. Then he rented two horses from Howard's stables on Seventh Street. The stage was set.

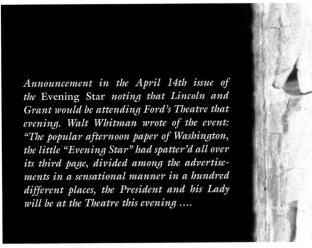
The afternoon newspapers created a public sensation by announcing that General and Mrs. Grant would accompany the Lincolns to Ford's Theatre that evening. Although the President was a familiar figure at the theater, having attended nearly a dozen performances there, Grant was almost a total stranger to the American public. Washingtonians eager for a glimpse of the victorious general bought every ticket to the evening performance, a sold-out show. Little did they know they were to witness one of the most memorable dramas in American history.

In honor of the Lincolns' attendance, theater manager Harry Clay Ford decorated the State Box with an appropriately patriotic display. Stagehand Edman (Ned) Spangler removed the partition between the two upper boxes to create a more spacious single box for the Presidential party. Two large American flags, each on a staff, festooned either side of the box, and two more flags draped the balustrades. The blue regimental flag of the United States Treasury Guards hung from a staff at the center pillar, and a framed engraving of George Washington completed the scene. Harry Ford supplied his personal black walnut rocking chair, upholstered in red damask, and a high-backed rush-seat chair for the President and First Lady; a smaller chair and a large red damask sofa accommodated the other guests.

While Booth and Harry Ford prepared the theater for the Lincolns' appearance that night, President and Mrs. Lincoln enjoyed a leisurely lunch together before setting off on a long afternoon carriage ride around the city. They stopped at the Navy Yard, where Lincoln visited the ironclad battleship, the *Montauk*.

When he returned to the White House, Lincoln passed a pleasant hour with Governor Oglesby and General Haynie, two of his Illinois friends. Between 7:30 and 8 p.m., Lincoln met with several visitors and well wishers before he excused himself to prepare for the theater. As the President and Mrs. Lincoln left the White House, already late for the show, former Massachusetts Representative George Ashmun unexpectedly called on the President. To assure Ashmun's appointment the next morning, Lincoln wrote on a card, "Allow Mr. Ashmun & friend to come in at 9 a.m. tomorrow. A. Lincoln. April 14, 1865." This was the last note Lincoln ever wrote.

Tickets from the April 14, 1865, performance at Ford's Theatre.

"Our American Cousin"

Despite the newspaper reports, General and Mrs. Grant declined the Lincolns' invitation to the theater that evening to visit their children in Burlington, New Jersey. Instead, Major Henry Rathbone and his fiancée, Miss Clara Harris, daughter of New York Senator Ira Harris, accompanied President and First Lady Lincoln to the theater that fateful night. The foursome rode the few blocks to Ford's Theatre for a performance of Tom Taylor's celebrated comedy, "Our American Cousin." The well-known actress Laura Keene starred as Florence Trenchard, her signature role that she had played more than 1,000 times. Keene was responsible for bringing the British play to the United States originally in 1858. Her co-star Harry Hawk played Asa Trenchard.

The performance was well under way when the Lincoln party arrived at the theater and climbed the curving stairway to the balcony. Noticing the President's arrival, Laura Keene stopped mid-sentence, and conductor William Withers, Jr., signaled the orchestra to strike up "Hail to the Chief." The audience rose in a thunderous standing ovation as Lincoln, the war hero of the hour, stepped to the front of the State Box and bowed in acknowledgment.

Once the party was seated—Lincoln in the rocker nearest the door to Box Seven, the First Lady next to him on a small black cane chair, Miss Harris on the high-backed chair in the far corner, and Major Rathbone to her left on the sofa—Act 1 resumed. Mary sat very close to her husband, her hand in his, gleaming in her black and white satin gown. She whispered to him, "What will Miss Harris think of my hanging on to you so?" The grinning President assured her, "She won't think anything about it."

Playbook and stage set of "Our American Cousin," the featured presentation at Ford's Theatre on the night of Lincoln's assassination.

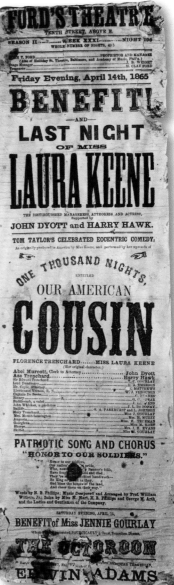

Clockwise from upper left: actress Laura Keene, actors John Dyott and Harry Hawk, advertisement for "Our American Cousin," actor T.C. Gourlay, orchestra conductor William Withers, Jr. and a violin thought to have been used in the orchestra on the night of Lincoln's assassination.

The President Is Shot!

Booth arrived at the theater shortly after the President settled into his rocking chair to enjoy the play, at around 9 p.m. He rode up Baptist Alley to the rear of the theater and called for stagehand Ned Spangler to hold his horse. Spangler was busy with the production, so he passed off the chore to "Peanuts" John Burroughs, a boy who worked odd jobs around the theater. Peanuts waited patiently for the next hour, unwittingly holding the reins of an assassin's escape horse.

Booth slipped into the theater for a final look around. He paced nervously in the main lobby, pausing every few moments to ask the doorman, John E. Buckingham, for the time. Twice Booth visited the Star Saloon next door and stiffened his resolve with several shots of whiskey as he waited for the appointed moment to arrive. At about ten minutes past ten, Booth returned to the theater and went up the circular stairs to the dress circle. As he

Above: John Wilkes Booth shot President Lincoln with this six-inch, single-shot derringer pistol.

Left: an artist's dramatic conception of Booth shooting the President.

approached the State Box, he presented a card of introduction to Charles Forbes, President Lincoln's personal messenger, who was sitting outside the State Box at the rear of the dress circle. Recognizing the well-known actor, Forbes admitted Booth.

Once inside the hallway, Booth placed the wooden brace against the door and approached the door to Box Seven. Through a hole in the door, he could see the President sitting in the rocking chair next to his wife, holding her hand and enjoying the show. Booth was familiar with the play and waited for a precise moment to make his move. On stage, the scheming widow Mrs. Mountchessington (Helen Muzzy) had just accused Asa Trenchard (Harry Hawk) of not knowing the manners of good society. She strutted off into the wings, leaving Trenchard alone on stage. "Don't know the manners of good society, eh?" he drawled. "Well, I guess I know enough to turn you inside out, old gal—you sockdologizing old mantrap!" The President was leaning slightly forward in the rocker with his hand on the balustrade, his head turned to watch the audience laughing gleefully at Trenchard's jibes.

Amid the audience's laughter, Booth, his six-inch, single-shot derringer in one hand, a dagger in the other, slipped silently into the box. Standing just behind the President, he took aim and fired point-blank at the back of Lincoln's head from just a few inches away. The bullet, less than a half-inch in diameter, entered slightly above Lincoln's left ear in the back of his head and lodged close behind his right eye. The President slumped forward and then fell backward in his chair, never to regain consciousness. Mary Lincoln grabbed her husband's body to keep him from falling.

After Booth shot Lincoln, he leaped from the State Box to the stage, twelve feet below. The confused audience did not realize that Lincoln had been shot; many thought the spectacle was part of the play.

Invited Guests That Did Not Attend
the Theater with the Lincolns

Fifteen people declined the Lincolns' invitation to join them at Ford's Theatre on the evening of April 14, 1865.

General & Mrs. U. S. Grant

The Washington papers had reported that the Grants would attend "Our American Cousin" with the Lincolns. However, shortly after the Cabinet meeting ended, Grant told the President that he and Mrs. Grant would be taking the 6:00 p.m. train to visit their children in New Jersey. They would be unable to attend the play with the Lincolns.

Mr. & Mrs. Edwin Stanton

Stanton was Lincoln's Secretary of War. Mr. Stanton was not a fan of the theater and Mrs. Stanton, like Mrs. Grant, did not get along well with Mrs. Lincoln, so the Stantons declined the invitation.

Thomas Eckert

Eckert was a telegraph officer in the War Department. Secretary of War Stanton denied Eckert permission to go to the theater because his presence was needed at work.

Schuyler Colfax

Colfax of Indiana was Speaker of the House of Representatives. He turned down the invitation because he was leaving for the Pacific coast the next morning.

George Ashmun

Ashmun of Massachusetts had presided over the 1860 Republican Convention, which had nominated Lincoln for President. He turned down the theater invitation because of a "previous engagement."

Richard J. Oglesby

Oglesby was governor of Illinois. He declined the invitation in order to visit other friends, but he told Lincoln he would be back to see him over the weekend.

Richard Yates

Yates was the ex-governor of Illinois. He excused himself from the invitation because he had other appointments with friends that evening.

FORD'S NEW THEATRE,
TENTH STREET, ABOVE PENNA. AVENUE.

BENEFIT AND LAST APPEARANCE
OF
MISS LAURA KEENE,
THIS (FRIDAY) EVENING, APRIL 14, 1865,
When she will appear as
FLORENCE TRENCHARD,
In her celebrated Comedy of
THE AMERICAN COUSIN,
From the original manuscript by Tom Taylor, as played at
LAURA KEENE'S THEATRE, NEW YORK,
For upwards of
THREE HUNDRED NIGHTS
She will be supported by
J. C. McCOLLOM, JOHN DYOTT, HARRY HAWK,
And the Entire Company.

TO-MORROW, BENEFIT OF MISS JEANNIE GOURLAY,
When will be presented the Great Drama, illustrative of
Southern Life. Southern Scenes, and Southern Homes,
Entitled
THE OCTOROON.

The popular young Tragedian, EDWIN ADAMS, is engaged for Twelve Nights only, and will appear on MONDAY, April 17th

General Isham N. Haynie

Haynie, a visitor from Illinois, had plans with other friends.

William A. Howard

Howard was the postmaster of Detroit. He had plans to leave Washington later that day.

Mr. & Mrs. William Wallace

Wallace was governor of the Idaho Territory. The couple declined the invitation, saying they were tired.

Noah Brooks

Brooks was a reporter friendly with Lincoln and his administration. He declined the Lincolns' invitation to the theater because he had a cold.

Robert Lincoln

The Lincolns' oldest son later said that as his parents were departing for Ford's, his father asked, "We're going to the theater, Bob, don't you want to go?" But Robert, just home from his tour of duty with General Grant, wanted to turn in early that night.

Source: Lincoln: An Illustrated Biography by Philip B. Kunhardt, Jr., Philip B. Kunhardt III, and Peter W. Kunhardt. Page 347.

"Sic Semper Tyrannis!"

Instantly Major Rathbone sprang upon the assassin. Booth dropped his gun, broke from Rathbone's grasp, and stabbed him almost to the bone of his left arm above the elbow. Booth placed one hand on the balustrade, raised his other arm to strike again at the advancing Rathbone, and vaulted over the railing. Rathbone caught only his coattail. As Booth leaped, his right boot struck the framed engraving of George Washington and his spur caught the fringe of the Treasury Guards' flag, pulling it down and tearing off a strip. The usually athletic Booth lost his balance and landed awkwardly on the stage twelve feet below. He fell forward on his hands and knees, fracturing a small bone in his left leg about two inches above the ankle.

Booth jumped to his feet and brandished his large knife, shouting to the confused audience, "Sic semper tyrannis!" ("Thus always to tyrants"—both the motto of the Commonwealth of Virginia and a line from the role of Shakespeare's Brutus)—before running across the stage. Harry Hawk, seeing Booth racing toward him with a knife, ran through the center doorway onstage and took refuge on a flight of stairs. Booth ran off the stage on the north side of the theater, between Laura Keene and young William Ferguson, who were standing beside the prompter's desk.

In the narrow aisle between the stage and the rear exit, Booth bumped into orchestra conductor William Withers, Jr., and slashed at him twice, cutting his coat and throwing him to the floor before rushing out the door. At the rear exit, he kicked "Peanuts" Burroughs in the chest, grabbed the waiting horse's reins, jumped into the saddle, and galloped down the alley into the black night.

Booth took advantage of the audience's confusion in the moments after he shot Lincoln to escape from the theater. He ran through the rear exit to the alley behind the theater, where his horse was waiting.

Attack on Seward

As Booth crept through Ford's Theatre toward the State Box at the appointed hour of 10 p.m., David Herold accompanied Lewis Powell to Secretary of State Seward's home on Lafayette Square near the White House. The secretary had been bedridden since April 5, when he had injured his jawbone and dislocated his collarbone in a carriage accident.

Powell was admitted to the secretary's residence on the pretense of delivering medicine for Seward. Carrying an 1858 Whitney Navy revolver and a huge silver-mounted bowie knife, Powell made his way past the butler, William H. Bell, and battled upstairs to Seward's bedroom, pistol-whipping Seward's son, Frederick, who attempted to block his way. When he reached the secretary's room, Powell jumped on the bed and slashed wildly at Seward, stabbing him three times. One stab wound went entirely through the secretary's right cheek. In all, Powell injured five people during his wild rampage before running from the house mumbling, "I'm mad! I'm mad!"

Herold was to wait for Powell and guide their escape from Washington, D.C., but when he heard the screams coming from the secretary's home, Herold did not wait as assigned, and rode off. Herold crossed the Navy Yard Bridge and escaped from Washington, leaving Powell to fend for himself. Powell spent the next two days hiding in a cemetery before returning to the Surratt boardinghouse near midnight on April 17. Police wagons outside the house apparently caused Powell some concern for Mary Surratt's well-being, so he went inside to check on her. When police questioned him, Powell said that Mrs. Surratt had hired him to dig a ditch for her, but she denied knowing him. Police arrested both suspects, and Seward's butler, William Bell, later identified Powell as Seward's attacker.

Seward was cut on both sides of his face, but Powell's thrusts had missed the vital arteries and spared his life. Seward survived the attack, and by fall his health had improved enough to return to work. His frail wife and daughter, however, never recovered from the shock of that frightful night. Mrs. Seward passed away two months after the attack, and his nineteen- year- old daughter Frances suffered nervous anxiety attacks for a year before she died in 1866. Seward carried horrible scars from the attack for the rest of his life, and refused any portraits except for one, in which his disfigured cheek is plainly visible.

After his recovery, Seward continued his duties as secretary of state under Lincoln's successor, President Andrew Johnson. In 1867, he resumed his impressive political career and negotiated the purchase of the Alaska territory from Russia for 7.2 million dollars, an acquisition then contemptuously referred to as "Seward's Folly." History redeemed him, however, in 1959, when Alaska became the forty-ninth state.

Secretary of State William Seward's home on Lafayette Square, across the street from the White House.

An artist's sketch of Powell forcing his way through Seward's home.

Conspirator George Atzerodt failed to carry out his assignment to kill Vice President Andrew Johnson. Instead, Atzerodt got drunk, lost his nerve, and fled north from Washington, knowing that Booth would head south. Likewise, Mike O'Laughlin, who returned from Baltimore on the day of the assassination for reasons that remain unclear, wandered drunkenly throughout Washington on the evening of April 14. Of the three attackers, only Booth succeeded in his sinister mission.

William Seward began his political career as state senator in Albany, New York, in 1830. From 1838 until 1842, he served as governor but then stepped aside, in part because his growing opposition to slavery had become a political liability. Seward entered the U.S. Senate in 1848 as a leading opponent of the extension of slavery into the western territories. As the Republican Party emerged in 1856, Seward joined its ranks, and when he failed to win the Republican nomination for President in 1860, he campaigned actively for Lincoln and became his Secretary of State. An able and successful diplomat, Seward deterred European entry in the Civil War, and after Lincoln's assassination, supported Lincoln's lenient plan for Reconstruction against opposing Radical Republicans. In 1867, Seward negotiated the sale of the Russian territory of Alaska to the United States for $7.2 million, or 2.5¢ per acre for an area twice the size of Texas.

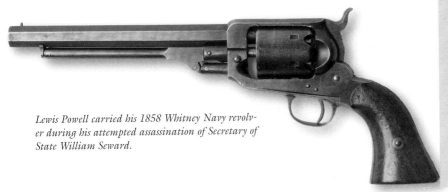

Lewis Powell carried his 1858 Whitney Navy revolver during his attempted assassination of Secretary of State William Seward.

The Aftermath

Throughout the night, anxious crowds gathered on the street outside and watched as Lincoln was carried from Ford's Theatre to the Petersen House across Tenth Street and waited for news about President Lincoln's condition, as soldiers (opposite) stood guard.

For a stunned moment, the audience at Ford's Theatre, not realizing what had happened, sat bewildered and confused. Many had not heard the gunshot above the laughter, and others assumed the entire spectacle was part of the play. Suddenly, Mrs. Lincoln's frantic screams alerted the audience that the President had been hurt, and as word spread throughout the hall, pandemonium broke out. Frantic crowds surged up and down the stairs and aisles. Women screamed and swooned. An anxious crowd outside the State Box rushed against the door, making it impossible for Rathbone to remove the brace jamming the door shut. Nearby audience members lifted several doctors up to the State Box, where the President sat slumped in his chair.

The first to reach Lincoln was twenty-three-year-old Assistant Surgeon Charles Augustus Leale, fresh out of Bellvue Hospital Medical College. The sandy-haired young man had come alone to the play that evening, just to catch a glimpse of the President, his hero. When he heard calls for a doctor, Leale leapt over the rows of chairs in front of him and rushed to the State Box. Once he saw the extent of the wound, Leale realized the futility of medical treatment. He laid Lincoln on the floor and restored his breathing, but declared, "His wound is mortal. It is impossible for him to recover."

Dr. Leale thought the bumpy carriage ride to the White House would probably kill the President and ordered him taken immediately to the closest available bed. After several soldiers emptied the theater, the unconscious President was carried down the main stairway to the lobby.

As they cleared a path through the anxious crowds outside, a young man called to them from the front stairs of a home almost directly across the street, "Bring him in here!" This young man was Henry S. Safford, a government clerk who lived at the Petersen boardinghouse. When he learned of the assassination from the crowds in the street, Safford immediately ran to the porch and summoned the soldiers. They carried the President up the curving stairs from the street and down the hall to the modest first-floor bedroom in the rear. Because the foot-board could not be removed, the small double bed had to be pulled away from the wall so the six-foot- four-inch Lincoln could be laid diagonally across it.

The nondescript brick house where Lincoln lay dying was owned by German emigrants William Petersen and his wife, Anna. They had settled in Washington in 1841 and built their home on Tenth Street eight years later. There, the couple and their six children lived in the basement, where Petersen also practiced his trade as a tailor. To supplement their income, the Petersens rented out the upper three levels to boarders, such as Henry Safford, the young man who beckoned the soldiers carrying President Lincoln from Ford's Theatre.

"Now He Belongs To The Ages"

Throughout the long deathwatch, Leale and nearly a dozen other doctors tended to President Lincoln in the back bedroom of the Petersen House. Surgeon General Joseph Barnes and Dr. Robert Stone, the Lincoln family physician, twice probed the President's wound but could not remove the bullet. Dr. Charles Leale held Lincoln's right hand throughout the night "to let him in his blindness know that he had a friend." All of Lincoln's Cabinet except two, Secretary of State Seward and Secretary of the Treasury McCullough, crowded into the small room, quietly watching as Lincoln slipped away.

The Cabinet met intermittently throughout the night in the rear parlor of the Petersen House, where Secretary of War Edwin M. Stanton began his investigation of the assassination. He closed Ford's Theatre, interviewed witnesses who easily identified Booth, and ordered his arrest. With the aid of Corporal James Tanner, a boarder from next door and a trained stenographer who tapped out important messages all night, Stanton relayed news of the President's approaching death around the world. Tanner, who had lost both legs in the Civil War, and Charles A. Dana, the assistant secretary of war, assisted Stanton throughout the night. They issued a statement and reward poster describing the assassin as "25 years old, 5 feet 8 inches tall, [with] dark hair and mustache. Use all efforts to secure him." Stanton released the news of the President's assassination to the press, and informed Vice President Andrew Johnson that he would be sworn in as President. Johnson visited President Lincoln's bedside once during the night, but departed before the end.

Supported by Major Rathbone, Clara Harris, and actress Laura Keene, Mary Lincoln followed her husband across the street to the Petersen House. Major Rathbone collapsed from blood loss in the hallway and was taken home. Mrs. Lincoln rested on a black horsehair sofa in the front parlor, where she lay inconsolable, moaning softly. When they heard the news, her son Robert, Lincoln's private secretary John Hay, and the family minister, the Reverend Dr. Phineas D. Gurley of the New York Avenue Presbyterian Church, joined her.

Twelve-year-old Tad, Lincoln's youngest son, was at Grover's National

Edwin McMasters Stanton

Born in Steubenville, Ohio, in 1814 to devout Methodist parents, Edwin Stanton developed a very successful legal career that attracted the attention of President James Buchanan, who appointed Stanton attorney general. President Lincoln appointed him secretary of war in 1862 to cleanse the department of notorious corruption. Stanton proved an able and honest administrator, consistently meeting demands for troops, weapons, and supplies. At Lincoln's death, Stanton uttered the memorable words, "Now he belongs to the ages." Stanton, vehemently opposed to President Andrew Johnson's lenient Reconstruction policies, led the battle to impeach Johnson. When Johnson attempted to fire Stanton in February 1868, he refused to leave office, claiming job protection under the Tenure of Office Act. Stanton later returned to private practice and was nominated to the Supreme Court on December 20, 1868. He died four days later.

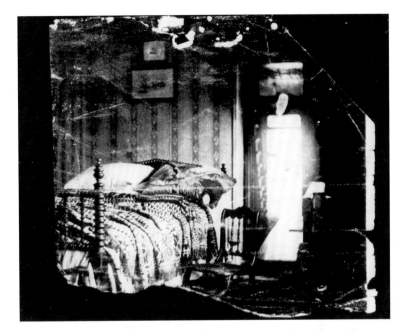

The photo on the right was taken by Petersen House boarder Julius Ulke just moments after Lincoln's body was removed. It has served as the basis for restorations and artistic renderings since its creation. News of Lincoln's death spread across the world. The engraving below shows Lincoln's deathbed scene as it appeared in a French broadside.

Theatre watching "Aladdin! Or His Magic Lamp" when his father was shot. A messenger whispered the news of the assassination to Alphonso Dunn, Tad's chaperone, who whisked away the boy. At the White House, doorman Tom Pendel tried to calm Tad's worried fears but could not put the boy to bed until near midnight. Once Tad had left Grover's, theater manager C. D. Hess interrupted the show to announce the shocking news of the tragedy to the audience.

When Abraham Lincoln was shot, he was carrying two pairs of spectacles and a lens polisher, a pocketknife, a watch fob, a linen handkerchief, and a brown leather wallet containing a five-dollar Confederate note and nine newspaper clippings, including several favorable to the President and his policies. Given to Robert Lincoln, these items were later donated to the Library of Congress in 1937.

Andrew Johnson

Born December 29, 1808, in Raleigh, North Carolina, Andrew Johnson grew up in poverty. His family apprenticed him to a tailor at age fourteen, but he ran away to Tennessee. There he established his own tailor shop and entered local politics. As an adept stump speaker championing the rights of the common man, he rose to prominence and was elected to five consecutive terms in the U.S. House of Representatives, served as the governor of Tennessee, and entered the U.S. Senate on the eve of the Civil War. In 1862, President Lincoln appointed Johnson as military governor of Tennessee, and nominated him as his running mate in the election of 1864. Johnson became President of the United States after Lincoln's death on April 15, 1865. A Southerner and a Democrat, Johnson's lenient plans for Reconstruction of the former Confederacy were contested by a radical faction of Republicans that eventually tried to impeach him. Johnson was acquitted by one vote. After his one term as President, Johnson remained active in Tennessee politics and was elected to the U.S. Senate in 1875. He died later that year and was buried in Greeneville, Tennessee, at what has become the Andrew Johnson National Historic Site.

At the Petersen House, Mrs. Lincoln was overwrought; she became increasingly hysterical as she visited her husband's bedside throughout the night. As she covered his face with kisses, Mary Lincoln begged her husband to wake one last time to speak with her and their children. After a particularly frantic bedside visit toward morning, she let out a piercing cry and fell in a faint to the floor. Secretary of War Edwin Stanton ordered gruffly, "Take that woman out and do not let her in again." Robert assisted his mother to the front parlor, as she wailed, "Oh, my God, I have given my husband to die." Mary Lincoln was not in the room when her husband passed away.

Lincoln struggled throughout the long night, his labored breathing the only sound in the silent room. By 11:30 p.m., his right eye was swollen and bruised. As a gray dawn lightened the room, his pulse gradually weakened, and at seven o'clock on the morning of April 15, Dr. Stone announced that death was near. At 7:22 a.m., Abraham Lincoln heaved a sigh and did not breathe again. Reverend Gurley offered a prayer and Secretary of War Edwin Stanton was said to quietly murmured the enduring words, "Now he belongs to the ages."

The Fate of the Rathbones

Henry Rathbone and Clara Harris accompanied the Lincolns to Ford's Theatre and witnessed the assassination. The couple married on July 11, 1867, and had three children. Rathbone suffered from "dyspepsia" or indigestion and severe mood swings and was probably taking an opiate to control his symptoms. (Opiates were used as medication and could be purchased over the counter in the nineteenth century.) The couple later moved to Germany. On December 23, 1883, Rathbone suffered a psychotic attack and tried to kill his children, shot and stabbed his wife to death, and finally stabbed himself. When the police arrived, Rathbone mumbled, "Who could have done this to my darling wife?" and raved about people "hiding behind the pictures on the wall." He spent the rest of his life in an asylum for the criminally insane in Hildesheim, Germany. He died on August 14, 1911, at the age of 73 and was buried in a small cemetery in Germany. It was destroyed by an Allied bombing raid during World War II.

Lincoln's Funeral

On the morning of April 15, Lincoln's body was placed in a simple coffin on a horse-drawn carriage and transferred through heavy rains to the White House. There doctors performed an autopsy, and Lincoln was laid in state in the East Room of the White House, eerily fulfilling his dream of several weeks prior. In the disturbing dream, Lincoln had recounted to his wife and his long-time friend and bodyguard, Ward Hill Lamon, that he heard the sound of loud sobbing, as if from a crowd. Following the sobs downstairs from his White House bedroom, he searched from room to room, but could not find the source of the weeping. Finally, he entered the East Room, where he saw a catafalque surrounded by guards and mourners. "Who is dead in the White House?" he asked. "The President," replied a soldier. "He was killed by an assassin." According to Lamon, Lincoln was noticeably shaken by this dream, just a few weeks before the fateful night at Ford's Theatre.

As in Lincoln's dream, a crowd of more than 600 government officials and dignitaries viewed Lincoln's open casket at the White House on April 18. After funeral services were held in the East Room on April 19, a procession of 100,000 mourners slowly followed the casket, mounted on a horse-drawn caisson, to the newly finished Capitol Rotunda. There, Lincoln's body lay in state for the next two days, as thousands of grief-stricken Americans filed by to pay their respects to their fallen leader.

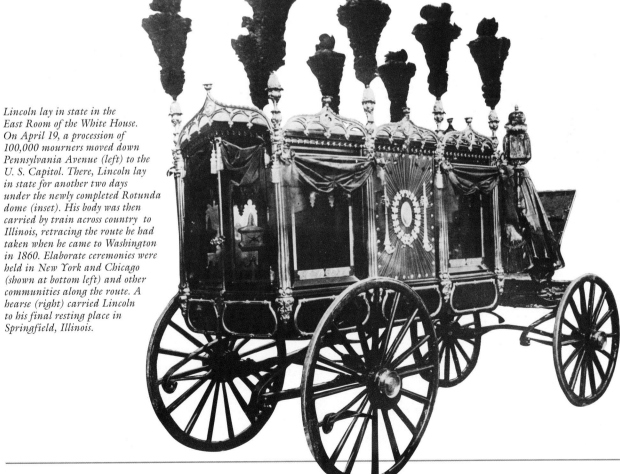

Lincoln lay in state in the East Room of the White House. On April 19, a procession of 100,000 mourners moved down Pennsylvania Avenue (left) to the U. S. Capitol. There, Lincoln lay in state for another two days under the newly completed Rotunda dome (inset). His body was then carried by train across country to Illinois, retracing the route he had taken when he came to Washington in 1860. Elaborate ceremonies were held in New York and Chicago (shown at bottom left) and other communities along the route. A hearse (right) carried Lincoln to his final resting place in Springfield, Illinois.

Lincoln's Funeral Train

On April 21, a week after the assassination, a special nine-car funeral train carrying the bodies of President Lincoln and his son Willie left Washington for Springfield, Illinois. Willie Lincoln had died in the White House from typhoid in 1862, and his body had been exhumed to accompany his father to Illinois. Lincoln's body was placed on view in ten cities along the route, where eulogies, ceremonies, funeral processions, and tolling bells demonstrated the nation's sorrow. At all hours of the day and night, in sun and pouring rain, farmers stood along stretches of the tracks, hats in their hands. Small towns offered cannon salutes as the train passed slowly by. Nearly seven million people, of a population of about thirty-two million at the time, paid their respects to the slain President. The funeral train reached Springfield, Illinois, on May 3, and Lincoln's body was placed in the black-draped State House for viewing. The next day, the casket was soldered shut and committed to the receiving vault of Oak Ridge Cemetery in Springfield.

The Lincoln Monument, built on a hill above the vault, was dedicated on October 15, 1874. Eventually, Mrs. Lincoln and three of their four sons, Edward, William, and Thomas (Tad) were buried there as well. Robert Todd Lincoln, the Lincolns' oldest son and the only one to reach adulthood, died in 1926 and is buried in Arlington National Cemetery.

Lincoln's body traveled on this train, in a decorated and guarded car (above right) from Washington, D.C., to Springfield, Illinois, where he was buried. The map (bottom right) shows the route of Lincoln's funeral train. Hundreds of thousands of mourners gathered in cities and along the tracks to pay their last respects.

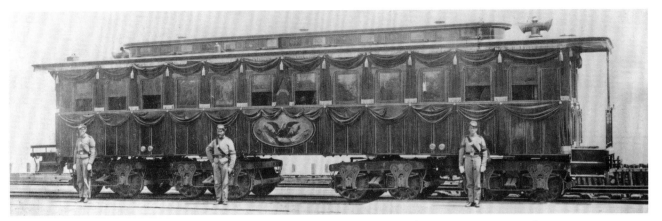

O Captain! My Captain!

WALT WHITMAN

"O Captain! My Captain!
our fearful trip is done;
The ship has weather'd every rack,
the prize we sought is won;
The port is near, the bells I hear,
the people all exulting,
While follow eyes the steady keel,
the vessel grim and daring:
But O heart! heart! heart!
O the bleeding drops of red,
Where on the deck my
Captain lies,
Fallen cold and dead.

O Captain! My Captain!
Rise up and hear the bells;
Rise up – for you the flag is flung
– for you the bugle trills;
For you bouquets and ribbon'd
wreaths –
for you the shores a-crowding;
For you they call, the swaying
mass,
their eager faces turning:
Here Captain! Dear father!
This arm beneath your head;
It is some dream that on the deck,
You've fallen cold and dead.

My Captain does not answer,
his lips are pale and still;
My father does not feel my arm,
he has no pulse or will;
The ship is anchor'd safe
and sound,
its voyage closed and done;
From fearful trip the victor ship
comes in with object won:
Exult, O shores, and ring, O bells!
But I with mournful tread,
Walk the deck my Captain lies,
Fallen cold and dead."

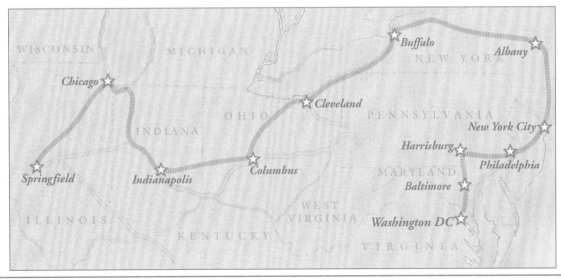

A Nation Mourns

Lincoln's tragic and sudden death at the height of celebration at the end of the war made him a national martyr almost immediately. Hundreds of Easter Sunday sermons paralleled the deaths of Lincoln and Christ, as saviors who suffered and died in atonement for the sins of mankind. Those who criticized Lincoln days before, now hailed him as the greatest of presidents. The nation had never witnessed such an outpouring of grief: black mourning crepe hung from every window and door; banners proclaimed the nation's loss; prayers, poems, songs and psalms praised the blessed martyr of freedom.

The country mourned Lincoln's death. Here the funeral cortege moves along a street in Philadelphia, while signs still are posted calling for new recruits to Major General Hancock's First Army Corps. At right, examples of memorabilia by which a grieving public paid tribute, now in the Lincoln collection at Ford's Theatre Museum.

The Fate of Mary Lincoln

Mary Lincoln was not well enough to attend many of her husband's funeral ceremonies, nor did she accompany the train on its long tour through the mourning country. For five weeks after the assassination, she remained mostly bedridden in the White House. Finally, on May 22, clothed entirely in black, Mary walked down the White House stairs for the last time. She, her seamstress and long-time friend Elizabeth Keckley, and her sons Robert and Tad boarded a train for Chicago. The President's widow never fully recovered from her terrible grief.

In May 1875, Robert Lincoln had his mother brought to trial on the charge of insanity. Judge Marion R. M. Wallace presided. After ten minutes of discussion, the jury found Mary Lincoln deranged and recommended that she be placed in an asylum. Mary was committed to Bellevue Place, a private sanitarium in Batavia, Illinois, for several months. Mary Lincoln traveled in Europe and lived with her older sister, Elizabeth, in Chicago. Mary Lincoln died on July 16, 1882, possibly from a stroke or complications from diabetes.

War Department, Washington, April 20. 1865.

$100,000 REWARD!

THE MURDERER

Of our late beloved President, ABRAHAM LINCOLN,

IS STILL AT LARGE.

$50,000 REWARD!

will be paid by this Department for his apprehension, in addition to any reward offered by Municipal Authorities or State Executives.

$25,000 REWARD!

will be paid for the apprehension of JOHN H. SURRATT, one of Booth's accomplices.

$25,000 REWARD!

will be paid for the apprehension of DANIEL C. HARROLD, another of Booth's accomplices.

LIBERAL REWARDS will be paid for any information that shall conduce to the arrest of either of the above-named criminals, or their accomplices.

All persons harboring or secreting the said persons, or either of them, or aiding or assisting their concealment or escape, will be treated as accomplices in the murder of the President and the attempted assassination of the Secretary of State, and shall be subject to trial before a Military Commission and the punishment of DEATH.

Let the stain of innocent blood be removed from the land by the arrest and punishment of the murderers.

All good citizens are exhorted to aid public justice on this occasion. Every man should consider his own conscience charged with this solemn duty, and rest neither night nor day until it be accomplished.

EDWIN M. STANTON, Secretary of War.

DESCRIPTIONS.—BOOTH is 5 feet 7 or 8 inches high, slender build, high forehead, black hair, black eyes, and wears a heavy black moustache.
JOHN H. SURRATT is about 5 feet 9 inches. Hair rather thin and dark; eyes rather light; no beard. Would weigh 145 or 150 pounds. Complexion rather pale and clear, with color in his cheeks. Wore light clothes of fine quality. Shoulders square; cheek bones rather prominent; chin narrow; ears projecting at the top; forehead rather low and square, but broad. Parts his hair on the right side; neck rather long. His lips are firmly set. A slim man.
DANIEL C. HARROLD is 23 years of age, 5 feet 6 or 7 inches high, rather broad shouldered, otherwise light built; dark hair, little (if any) moustache; dark eyes; weighs about 140 pounds.

GEO. F. NESBITT & CO., Printers and Stationers, cor. Pearl and Pine Streets, N. Y.

Flight from Justice

During the chaos following the assassination, Booth fled down F Street to Pennsylvania Avenue and crossed the Navy Yard Bridge. The posted sentry at the bridge had been instructed not to let anyone cross after the 9 p.m. curfew, but the recent end of the war and Booth's refined appearance lowered his guard. The same soldier allowed David Herold, who had fled from Secretary of State Seward's house, to leave Washington via the bridge about fifteen minutes later. Herold caught up with Booth and they continued together to Surratt's Tavern, where they recovered some whiskey, a carbine, and Booth's field glasses.

Around 4 a.m. on April 15, as Lincoln struggled with his last breaths, the fugitives reached the home of Dr. Samuel Mudd in

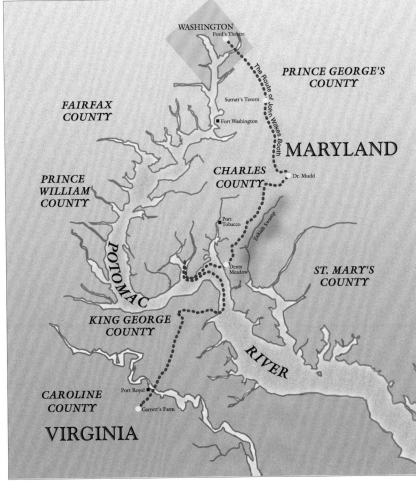

The map above outlines their escape route. Opposite page: Secretary of War Edwin Stanton issued a reward poster for the capture of the "murderer" John Wilkes Booth and his two accomplices, John Surratt and David Herold, erroneously named Daniel Harrold.

This compass directed Booth and Herold south from Washington to Port Royal, Virginia.

southern Maryland. Mudd set Booth's injured left leg, gave him an old pair of crutches, and allowed the two men to rest for several hours. Mudd would later admit this assistance, but maintained that he did not know who his patient was. It is known, however, that the two men had met before on at least three separate occasions.

The fugitives resumed their flight later that afternoon and arrived by midnight at the home of Samuel Cox, a Confederate supporter, near Zekiah Swamp, within a few miles of the Potomac River. Cox's foster brother, Thomas Jones, another Confederate signal agent, supplied the men with food and newspapers, while they hid out in a nearby pine

This engraving shows David Herold and John Wilkes Booth crossing the Potomac River from Maryland to the Virginia shore.

The Surratt House and Museum

Built in 1852 as a middle-class plantation home, the historic Surratt House served as a tavern and hostelry, a post office, and a polling place in the 1850s. During the Civil War, Surratt's tavern was a safehouse for the Confederate underground, which flourished in southern Maryland. Today, the museum presents a variety of programs and events, recapturing the spirit of mid-nineteenth century life and focusing on the fascinating conspiracy story. The Surratt House and Museum is located in Clinton, Maryland, twelve miles southeast of Washington, D.C.

thicket for five days, often within yards of their pursuers. Here, cold, hungry, and dirty, Booth huddled in a ditch and recorded in his datebook his profound disappointment with the public reaction to the assassination. He had "struck boldly... and walked with a firm step" as the nation had demanded, yet his deed was condemned as the most heinous of crimes. "I am here in despair," he wrote, "And why? For doing what Brutus was honored for. And yet I, for striking down a greater tyrant than they ever knew, am looked upon as a common cutthroat. I cannot see my wrong, except in serving a degenerate people. The little, the very little, I left behind to clear my name, the Government will not allow to be printed. So ends all. For my country I have given up all that makes life sweet and holy, brought misery upon my family, and am sure there is no pardon in the Heaven for me, since man condemns me so."

Booth carried this 1864 datebook, which he used as a diary, on his flight through Maryland and Virginia.

Booth also carried a compass (seen on page 73), a whistle, keys, photographs of five women, and a knife when the military overtook him in Virginia.

Manhunt and Capture

As Booth and Herold hid in the pine thickets of southern Maryland, thousands of outraged citizens joined detectives, police, and militia to track down the fugitives. Cavalry troops advanced in all directions, blocking roads and searching homes as they went. It was assumed that Booth would head south in search of protection in the old Confederacy, so about 2,000 cavalry troops descended on southern Maryland, searching for the assassin. Booth and Herold could hear the pounding of nearby hoof-beats as they hid in the woods.

After five days of taking cover, Thomas Jones judged it safe to guide Booth and Herold to the Maryland banks of the Potomac River. On the morning of April 23, Jones provided directions and a rickety rowboat for their journey to the Virginia shore. Once in Virginia, reluctant locals and three Confederate soldiers directed Booth and Herold to the home of Richard H. Garrett, near Port Royal. There, ninety-five miles from Ford's Theatre, their pursuers finally caught up with them.

At about 2 a.m. on April 26, a twenty-six-man cavalry detachment under Lieutenant Colonel E. J. Conger tracked Booth and Herold to Garrett's farm. When soldiers placed a rope around his father's neck, young Jack Garrett did not hesitate to reveal the hiding place of the two men. The soldiers stealthily surrounded the barn where Booth and Herold slept.

Conger called to the fugitives,

An artist's rendering of the capture of the assassin, John Wilkes Booth, in Port Royal, Virginia. Booth was trapped in a burning barn and shot on April 26, 1865, twelve days after he shot President Lincoln.

"We know who you are. Surrender yourselves!" After a few minutes of discussion with Booth, Herold willingly surrendered, leaving the barn hands held aloft, but Booth refused to give up without a fight. To force him out, Colonel Conger set the building on fire. As the crackling flames reached the dry wooden roof, Booth hesitated, unsure of his next move. A soldier named Thomas "Boston" Corbett recalled later that as the flames consumed the building, he saw Booth lift his rifle. Against orders, Private Corbett fired first as "Providence directed" him, and shot Booth clean through the neck. Booth dropped his carbine and fell heavily forward. The soldiers dragged the wounded fugitive out of the burning barn and laid him on Richard Garrett's front porch. Paralyzed, Booth lingered for three hours, and when asked for his last words said, "Tell mother I died for my country." Booth died at 5:30 a.m., twelve days after his own bullet had brought down the final curtain on the life of Abraham Lincoln.

In contrast to Lincoln's grand funeral procession, Booth's body was transferred secretly to the Washington Navy Yard in a gunny sack, where it was autopsied, identified, and buried hastily on April 27, beneath a cell in the Washington Penitentiary. When the penitentiary was demolished in October 1867, Booth's remains were removed to the nearby arsenal warehouse. His body remained there until it was released to his family two years later. The Booths buried him on June 26, 1869, in the family plot in Green Mount Cemetery in Baltimore, Maryland.

Thomas "Boston" Corbett

At the outbreak of the Civil War, Thomas P. ("Boston") Corbett eagerly joined the Union army and re-enlisted three times before finally becoming a sergeant in the Sixteenth New York Cavalry. Corbett was captured on June 24, 1864, in Centreville, Virginia, and spent time in Andersonville Prison.

In April 1865, the Sixteenth New York Cavalry tracked John Wilkes Booth to Richard Garrett's tobacco shed near Port Royal, Virginia. Corbett shot Booth with a Colt revolver through a large crack in the barn. He said that "God Almighty directed" him to kill Booth, although in his official statement of May 1, 1865, Corbett claimed he shot Booth because he thought the fugitive intended to open fire. Corbett was placed under technical arrest, but Secretary of War Stanton dropped the charges saying, "The rebel is dead. The patriot lives."

Corbett spent his last years in a seemingly delusional state. In the late 1880s, overhearing a derisive comment about a prayer, he brandished his revolver at the "heretics." Corbett was arrested, declared psychotic, and imprisoned in the Topeka Asylum for the Insane.

On May 26, 1888, Corbett escaped from the asylum. Although a few stories have surfaced, there is no proof that Boston Corbett was ever heard from again. His fate remains a mystery.

Trial and Sentencing

The authorities quickly rounded up Booth's fellow conspirators following Lincoln's assassination. On April 17, police arrested Mary Surratt at her H Street boardinghouse. She had "kept the nest that hatched the egg," according to President Andrew Johnson. Lewis Powell walked into the Surratt boardinghouse while the police were there, and he was also arrested. Samuel Arnold and Michael O'Laughlin, Booth's old school friends who had fled north after the failed kidnapping attempt, were apprehended three days after the shooting. George Atzerodt, who had conspired to kill Vice President Andrew Johnson, and Dr. Samuel Mudd, the Maryland doctor who set Booth's leg, were taken into custody on April 21. John Surratt, who was in Elmira, New York, at the time of the assassination, fled to Canada and later to Europe when he heard news of the murder.

Samuel Arnold, George Atzerodt, David Herold, Dr. Samuel Mudd, Michael O'Laughlin, Lewis Powell, Edman (Ned) Spangler and Mary Surratt were imprisoned at the Washington Penitentiary under heavy guard. They were kept in separate cells under constant watch, never by the same guard twice. All but Mary Surratt and Dr. Mudd were made to wear heavy canvas hoods with a small nose and mouth hole, but no eye holes. The four conspirators were brought to trial before a military commission on May 9, 1865. On July 5, the commission found the conspirators guilty as charged, and they were hanged in the penitentiary yard (now Fort Lesley J. McNair) on July 7, 1865.

The execution of Mrs. Mary Surratt, the first woman put to death by the U.S. Government, caused an enormous public uproar. Until the end, Lewis Powell maintained that Mrs. Surratt was innocent, and most believed that her sentence would be commuted to life imprisonment. She was convicted on the testimony of John Lloyd, who leased her tavern in Surrattsville, Maryland, and Louis Weichmann, her boarder.

According to these witnesses, on April 11, 1865, Mrs. Surratt traveled to Surrattsville with Louis Weichmann. Along the way, they met John Lloyd on the road at Uniontown. Lloyd testified that Mrs. Surratt told him that the "shooting irons" that had been hidden in Lloyd's tavern by Booth's co-conspirators would be needed soon. Three days later, on the day of the assassination, Mrs. Surratt made another trip to Surrattsville. Again Weichmann accompanied her in a hired buggy. This time, according to Lloyd, she delivered Booth's French field glasses and reminded him to ready the weapons and escape gear hidden at the tavern. Mary Surratt claimed total innocence. She said she knew nothing of Booth's assassination plans, and that her trips to Surrattsville were made to collect some money she was owed by a man named John Nothey.

Of the nine men of the military jury that convicted Mary Surratt and recommended the death penalty, five men added a plea for clemency due to Surratt's "sex and age." They suggested that the penalty be changed to life in prison. President Johnson later swore that he was never informed of this appeal. Some historians continue to debate the extent of Mary Surratt's involvement in Booth's plan to assassinate President Lincoln.

The executed conspirators were buried on the grounds of the arsenal until 1869, when President Andrew Johnson authorized the release of the bodies to their families. Mary Surratt is buried in Mt. Olivet Cemetery in Washington, D.C.; Lewis Thorton Powell is buried in a family plot in Geneva, Florida; David Herold is buried in Congressional Cemetery in Washington, D.C.; and George Atzerodt is buried in Druid Hill Park in Baltimore, Maryland.

Dr. Mudd, Samuel Arnold, and Michael O'Laughlin, who refused to participate in the assassination conspiracy, received sentences of life imprisonment at Fort Jefferson on the Dry Tortugas, west of Key West, Florida. There, O'Laughlin died of yellow fever in 1867, and President Johnson fully pardoned Dr. Mudd and Arnold in February 1869.

Disputes over the extent of Dr. Mudd's guilt persist to this day. It seems clear that he intended to assist Booth in transporting the captured President to Virginia, but no evidence has linked Mudd to

Conspirators Lewis Powell, David Herold, George Atzerodt, and Mary Surratt were hanged in the Washington Penitentiary yard on July 7, 1865.

Dr. Samuel Alexander Mudd

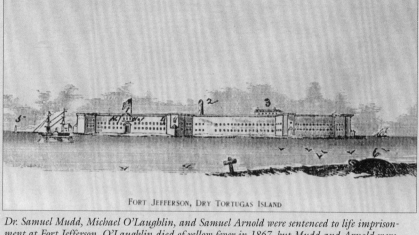

FORT JEFFERSON, DRY TORTUGAS ISLAND

Dr. Samuel Mudd, Michael O'Laughlin, and Samuel Arnold were sentenced to life imprisonment at Fort Jefferson. O'Laughlin died of yellow fever in 1867, but Mudd and Arnold were released by President Johnson in 1869.

Samuel Alexander Mudd was born on December 20, 1833, on a large plantation in Charles County, Maryland. He was well educated, attending St. John's College in Frederick, Maryland, Georgetown College in Washington, D.C., and graduating from the University of Maryland in 1856 with a medical degree. Dr. Mudd returned home and began life as a practicing physician and farmer. He married his childhood sweetheart, Sarah Frances Dyer, and the couple had four children. By 1859 the Mudds had a farm of their own located about thirty miles south of Washington, D.C. On Sunday, November 13, 1864, John Wilkes Booth first met Dr. Mudd at St. Mary's Church near Bryantown, Maryland. Mudd's involvement in the capture plot of Abraham Lincoln is unclear, but Mudd provided rest and medical treatment for Booth after Booth assassinated the President. At his trial, Mudd was found guilty and sentenced to life imprisonment at Ft. Jefferson in the Dry Tortugas, about seventy miles from Key West. He was spared the death penalty by only one vote. In the summer of 1867, when yellow fever broke out, Mudd aided the sick and dying prisoners. Because of his outstanding efforts, the soldiers on the island signed a petition on his behalf. On February 8, 1869, he was pardoned by President Andrew Johnson and returned home to Maryland. Dr. Mudd died in 1883 of pneumonia or pleurisy at the age of forty-nine and was buried in St. Mary's cemetery, next to the Bryantown church where he first met John Wilkes Booth.

Dr. Mudd's surgical tools (left) and John Wilkes Booth's boot, which was cut away from his broken leg on the morning after the assassination. Both are exhibited at the Lincoln Museum at Ford's Theatre.

the assassination plot. Many historians believe that when Booth and Herold arrived at his farm early on April 15, 1865, Dr. Mudd had no knowledge of what had happened at Ford's Theatre the night before. Mudd's relatives have spent decades trying to clear the family name.

Edman (Ned) Spangler, the stagehand whom Booth asked to hold his getaway horse, was charged with aiding and abetting Booth's escape and sentenced to six years in prison. President Johnson pardoned Spangler in 1869.

John Surratt, who was in Elmira, New York, at the time of the assassination, fled to Canada when he heard the news of Lincoln's murder. From there, he escaped to England and later to Rome. He joined the Papal Zouaves, but escaped again to Alexandria, Egypt, when his whereabouts were discovered. Finally, Surratt was arrested in Egypt on November 27, 1866, and returned to the United States. On June 10, 1867, Surratt was tried in Washington by a civil court. His trial ended in a hung jury, and he went free in the summer of 1868.

John Surratt, dressed in the elaborate uniform of the Papal Zouaves.

Dr. Samuel Mudd House and Museum

Dr. Samuel Mudd's home in Bryantown, Maryland, has been preserved by the famous doctor's descendents. The house museum, gift shop, kitchen, exhibit building and outbuildings, located on ten acres, are open for tours during summer weekends. Special exhibits, such as pictures of President Lincoln and clothing of the period, are shown periodically in the kitchen. Civil War encampments have been held on the grounds.

During the long night of April 14-15, 1865, the back parlor of the three-story brick Petersen House, across Tenth Street from Ford's Theatre, served as the seat of the United States government while Secretary of War Stanton endeavored to provide the necessary leadership following Lincoln's assassination. Government officials took over the parlor and the adjoining room, which home furnishings dealer George Francis and his wife rented at the time. From the round center table in the parlor, Stanton directed Cabinet meetings, conducted interrogations, ordered the seizure of Ford's Theatre and the arrest of John T. Ford and his employees, and directed the manhunt for John Wilkes Booth and his accomplices. Stanton questioned a handful of eyewitnesses who identified Booth as the assassin, ordered that the news of Lincoln's death be telegraphed to the country, and notified Vice President Andrew Johnson that Johnson would succeed Abraham Lincoln as President of the United States.

The Petersen House

Today, the front parlor of the Petersen House has been refurbished in a style similar to its 1865 appearance, although none of the original furniture remains. The double doors that separated the front parlor from the bedroom have been removed, creating one large room. Otherwise, the rooms appear much as they did in 1865.

Lincoln died in the rear first floor bedroom, at that time rented by William T. Clark, a young soldier in the Massachusetts Infantry. According to most accounts, Clark was out on the town, celebrating the imminent end of the Civil War, when history was made in his room. This bedroom has been faithfully restored to its appearance of that night, thanks to a photograph taken by another boarder, Julius Ulke, minutes after the President's body was removed. Some of the pieces are replicas based on the Ulke photograph; others are period pieces representing the typical examples of mid-nineteenth-century furnishings.

The ordeal brought unwelcome publicity to the Petersens and their boarders. Throngs of sightseers and souvenir seekers cut up the carpets, curtains, and bloodstained sheets from the back bedroom. Tourists regularly visited the house, gathering outside on the sidewalk and hoping to catch a glimpse of the room where Lincoln died. Eventually the boarders moved and Petersen's business failed. By 1870, only three Petersen children and one boarder remained in the house with William and Anna. Both of the elder Petersens died in 1871.

In 1878, the Petersen heirs sold the house and its furnishings to settle the estate. Mr. and Mrs. Louis Schade bought the house for $4,500, and lived there for several years. Schade was a prominent German-American lawyer who published the *Washington Sentinel* from the basement of the house. During their ownership, the Schades made several additions to the house, but left the historic rooms much as they were in 1865. They consented to identify the home with a marble tablet, which Congress authorized and donated in 1883. (A bronze marker replaced it in 1924.) Eventually, persistent tourists drove the Schades to move out and rent the property to the Memorial Association of the District of Columbia. The Association invited Osborn H. I. Oldroyd, a well-known collector of Lincoln memorabilia, to occupy the house as custodian.

Oldroyd began collecting memorabilia during Lincoln's election campaign in 1860. In 1883, he rented the Lincolns' Springfield, Illinois, home and lived there until he was called to Washington to oversee the Petersen House in 1893. By this time, his extensive collection numbered more than 3,000 objects related to Lincoln's life and political career. In 1896, the Federal Government bought the Petersen house from the Schade family for $30,000 and retained Oldroyd as the live-in custodian. The Petersen House was the first historic house bought by the Government solely for museum purposes.

The restored parlor of the Petersen House where Secretary of War Edwin Stanton and other officials directed the affairs of government.

The History of Ford's Theatre 1865-1933

Immediately after Lincoln's assassination, Secretary of War Edwin Stanton closed Ford's Theatre and canceled all scheduled dramatic productions during his investigation of the assassination. John Ford was in Richmond on the night of the assassination, visiting relatives. He did not know of the tragedy at his theater until he boarded a steamer for Baltimore the next morning. He was arrested on April 18 and spent thirty-nine days in prison, all the while Ford's Theatre remained closed.

The Federal Government returned the now infamous building to John Ford when he received official permission to reopen it on July 7, 1865. Ever the entrepreneur, Ford advertised yet another grand reopening. This time, however, his announcement aroused enormous public outrage, threats of arson, and other anonymous violent threats warning him to shut down for good. Fearing bloodshed, Secretary Stanton seized Ford's Theatre again, and Ford began a lengthy legal battle to retain ownership or receive compensation.

When Ford threatened to sue, the Federal Government agreed to rent the building for $1,500 per month until June 1, 1866, with the option to buy it for $100,000. Congress provided these funds in the Deficiency Appropriation Acts of July 7, 1865 and April 7, 1866.

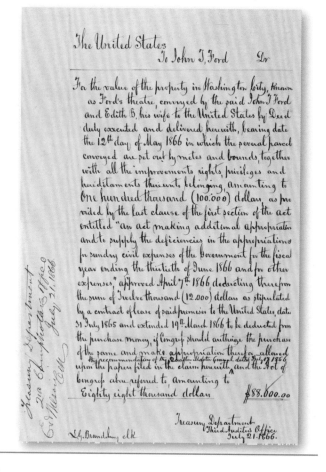

When Ford attempted to reopen his infamous theater, he received threatening letters from the public. Finally, the Federal Government bought the property in July 1866.

Ford's Theatre in September 1865, in an early phase of remodeling for use as a government office building. This and other photos, some made by famed Civil War photographer Mathew Brady, have served as the basis for authentication of details in the rebuilding of Ford's Theatre by the National Park Service. Total cost for restoration has been estimated at $2,760,000 – including the original engineering study, construction, furnishings, a sound and light program, and museum exhibits.

Government Ownership

As the new proprietor of Ford's Theatre, the Federal Government initiated an extensive renovation plan. The government awarded a $28,500 contract to a New York firm to restructure the historic theater into office and storage space. Workers removed the ornate woodwork and decorative plaster on the stage and balconies, dismantled the gas fixtures and stage boxes, and divided the building into three floors. Some of the interior decor was sent to Ford's Holliday Street Theatre in Baltimore, but the remaining furnishings were destroyed or lost.

By November 27, 1865, the renovations were complete, and the War Department's Record and Pension Bureau occupied the space beginning in April 1866. Several other government offices were housed in the building, including the Army Medical Museum, located on the third floor between 1867 and 1887.

Catastrophe again visited the historic building on the morning of June 9, 1893. The faulty construction of the east facade suddenly gave way, and the three upper floors supporting heavy office equipment collapsed into the basement. A seating chart now displayed in the Lincoln Museum indicates where employees of the Pension Bureau were seated at the moment of the disaster. A photograph of Howard S. Miller, a government clerk killed in the accident, and a list of other victims memorializes the twenty-two dead and sixty-eight injured government employees.

Despite this tragedy, the building was once again repaired and reopened the following year as an office building and storage facility for the War Department.

On July 1, 1928, the War Department transferred ownership of the building to the Office of Public Buildings and Public Parks of the National Capital. This office was absorbed by the National Park Service on June 10, 1933.

Ford's Theatre (opposite page) was gutted and transformed into government office space in late 1865. The Record and Pension Bureau of the War Department was housed here from 1865 until 1893.

A ceramic floor tile (above right) commemorates the tragic building collapse in 1893 (shown in lower photographs) that killed twenty-two and injured sixty-eight federal employees.

Restoration of Ford's Theatre

On February 6, 1946, Senator Milton R. Young of North Dakota, encouraged by Melvin Hildreth, a prominent Washington attorney and a fellow North Dakotan, introduced Joint Resolution 139 to the U.S. Senate. Senator Young's bill directed the Secretary of the Interior to prepare an estimate for the cost of reconstructing Ford's Theatre to its appearance on the evening of April 14, 1865. Over the next two decades, Young spearheaded the effort in Congress to restore this "great historic shrine" to its former glory. Thanks to Young's hard work, President Dwight D. Eisenhower signed the resolution into law on May 28, 1954. When the impending Civil War centennial aroused public interest in the restoration, Congress appropriated an additional $200,000 for research in 1960, and another $2 million dollars in 1964 for construction costs. On November 29, 1964, Ford's Theatre closed for a full restoration.

Three years of extensive restorations followed. Except for a few items, all the interior furnishings throughout the theater are exact reproductions based on contempo-

This original engraving of George Washington hung on the State Box on the evening Lincoln was assassinated.

rary photographs, sketches, drawings, newspaper articles, official reports, and samples of wallpaper and curtain fabric from museum collections. The outside walls of the theater were reinforced, and the interior was painstakingly reconstructed to conform to its appearance on the night John Wilkes Booth assassinated President Lincoln. Modern additions included climate control, fire and safety code precautions, and larger seats for the audience.

The State Box, also called the Presidential Box, has been reconstructed to look as it did on the night of Lincoln's assassination. The furniture and flags in the box were duplicated especially for the restoration, except for the crimson damask sofa and the framed engraving of George Washington, which are originals. Descendents of the Ford family donated both items in the 1940s. The original blue Treasury Guards' flag that draped the front of the box, and which Booth tore with his spur, is displayed in the downstairs museum. The rocking chair is a reproduction of the original in which Lincoln sat; the original is in the Henry Ford Museum in Dearborn, Michigan. The small black chair where Mary Lincoln sat is also a copy based on the original, currently housed at the Chicago Historical Society. The remaining two chairs, the four American flags, and the drapes were reproduced based on photographs by Mathew Brady and similar artifacts of the time.

Very few pieces of the interior structure or furnishings remain from the orginal Ford's Theatre. A piece of decorated glass (above) from the building is on display at the Lincoln Museum at Ford's Theatre.

From late 1964 through 1967, Ford's Theatre underwent extensive restorative work to return the historic playhouse to its lavish appearance on the evening of President Lincoln's assassination.

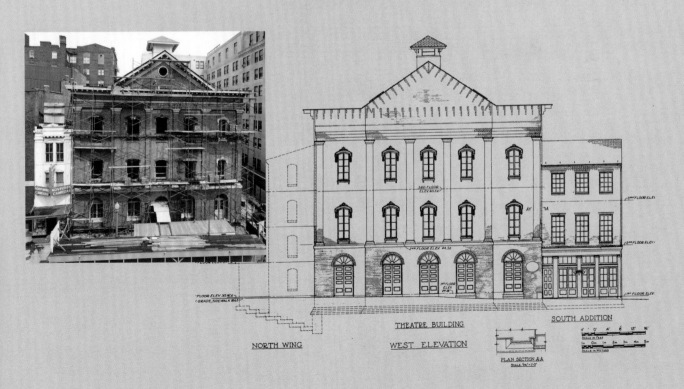

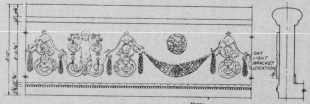

DRESS CIRCLE SECTION   FAMILY CIRCLE   SECTION

INTERPRETATION FROM PHOTOGRAPHS OF REPEATING DESIGN ON BALCONY RAILS

Architects, historians, and craftspeople meticulously studied available sources to restore Ford's Theatre to its 1865 appearance. Intricately detailed ornamentation, the ornate ceiling, and the grand sweep of the balconies recall the nineteenth-century design.

Opposite page: the restored facade of Ford's Theatre.

A Theatre Reborn

After more than three years of extensive reconstruction work, on January 21, 1968, Senator Young had the pleasure of presiding over the dedication of the historic theater to the memory of Abraham Lincoln. "Now," said Senator Young, "for those who revere Lincoln, a visit to the restored Ford's Theatre will be an unforgettable experience."

Indeed, the grand reopening and dedication at Ford's Theatre on January 30, 1968, was a memorable occasion. Ten of America's best known performing artists participated in a nationally televised celebration. First Lady of the American Stage, Helen Hayes, was the first performer to set foot on the stage. She was accompanied by Henry Fonda, Frederic March, and Robert Ryan as narrators for the special program of dance, opera, folk music, comedy, and dramatic verse dedicated to President Lincoln's love for the performing arts. Harry Belafonte sang "The Battle Hymn of the Republic;" Andy Williams performed popular tunes of Lincoln's day; poets read the verses of William Shakespeare and Walt Whitman; Herb Shriner

devoted a piece to Lincoln's well-known sense of humor, and Odetta performed a medley of African-American spirituals. More than one hundred years had passed since the night President Abraham Lincoln was shot watching "Our American Cousin" from his balcony seat. Yet in a fitting gesture to President Lincoln, who loved the performing arts, a new generation reclaimed Ford's Theatre as a national memorial to a fallen leader, and returned it to the public as a living theater.

Helen Hayes on stage at the grand reopening and dedication of Ford's Theatre on January 30, 1968.

Ford's Theatre opened to the public for the first time in 103 years on February 13, 1968, with Stephen Vincent Benét's Pulitzer Prize-winning play, "John Brown's Body." After more than a century of silence, Ford's Theatre had returned to the world of entertainment and art that President Lincoln had so enjoyed.

Today, the Ford's Theatre Society continues to produce musicals and plays that exemplify family values, underscore multiculturalism, and illuminate the diversity of American life. Ford's Theatre concentrates on presenting new American musicals and is one of only a few theaters in Washington capable of providing a national venue for large-scale productions. Ford's also promotes "American originals," plays about Americans whose lives and accomplishments have enriched the cultural fabric of our nation. Plays run September – June with scheduled matinees and evening shows. When shows or rehearsals are not in progress, visitors are welcome to explore the auditorium, view the restored Presidential Box, and experience the theater's dramatic history in a nineteenth-century setting.

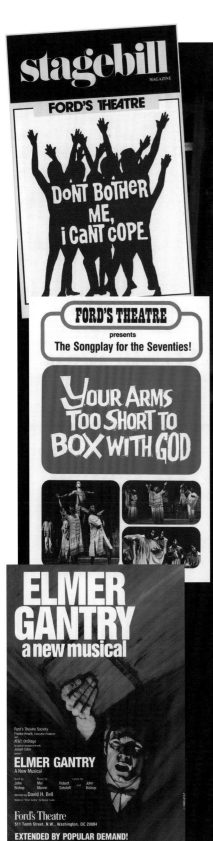

stagebill
MAGAZINE

FORD'S THEATRE

DON'T BOTHER ME, I CAN'T COPE.

FORD'S THEATRE
presents
The Songplay for the Seventies!

YOUR ARMS TOO SHORT TO BOX WITH GOD

ELMER GANTRY
a new musical

Ford's Theatre Society
Frankie Hewitt, *Executive Producer*
and
AT&T: OnStage
by special arrangement with
Joseph Colko

ELMER GANTRY
A New Musical

Book by   Music by   Lyrics by
John   Mel   Robert   and   John
Bishop   Marvin   Satuloff   Bishop

Directed by David H. Bell

Based on "Elmer Gantry" by Special Credit

Ford's Theatre
511 Tenth Street, N.W., Washington, DC 20004

EXTENDED BY POPULAR DEMAND!

To-Night!
Mr. Harry Hawk's COMPANY
SPECIAL ENGAGEMENT!!!
ONLY LOCAL APPEARANCE!

A sizzling musical full of explosive dance...
cool jazz, rousing gospel and 40's swing.

HOT MIKADO

Production made possible by a grant from AT&T.

Ford's Theatre

EXTENDED BY POPULAR DEMAND!
JOE SEARS & JASTON WILLIAMS
THE STARS OF
GREATER TUNA
& A TUNA CHRISTMAS
IN THE WORLD'S FAVORITE MUSICAL

The Fantasticks

MUSIC BY
HARVEY SCHMIDT

BOOK & LYRICS BY
TOM JONES

JULY 28TH

Since 1968, Ford's Theatre has presented a variety of American plays and musicals. Among them, "Reunion," a play dramatizing the events surrounding Lincoln's assassination, was presented by a fictitious "Mr. Harry Hawk's Company."

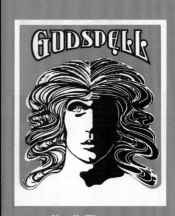

GODSPELL

Ford's Theatre

The Lincoln Museum

Osborn Oldroyd's 3,000-piece collection of Lincoln memorabilia had served as an informal exhibit at the Petersen House since 1893, when he was hired as curator of the historic house. However, in 1926, U.S. Representative Henry Rathbone of Illinois, the son of the couple who witnessed Lincoln's assassination in the State Box on the night of April 14, 1865, introduced a bill to purchase Oldroyd's Lincoln collection for $50,000. Two years later, ownership of the Petersen House and Ford's Theatre was transferred to the Office of Public Buildings and Public Parks of the National Capital.

When the doors of Ford's Theatre reopened to the public as the Lincoln Museum on the anniversary of President Lincoln's birthday in 1932, Oldroyd's collection served as the core of the museum. Pictorial exhibits on the first floor told the story of Lincoln's life and Presidency. A model of the theater and some photographs gave visitors an impression of the appearance of the interior at the time of Lincoln's assassination, and black outlines on the floor marked the approximate locations of the stage and the State Box where the Lincolns and their guests were sitting. Footprints on the floor indicated John Wilkes Booth's escape route from the theater after he shot President Lincoln.

Both the size and the focus of the Lincoln Museum have evolved since that time. What began as Oldroyd's private collection of varied

Opposite: The Lincoln Museum as it looked when it was housed at the Petersen House in 1909.

Right: Osborn Oldroyd, Lincoln memorabilia collector and long-time custodian of the Petersen House.

Below: The Lincoln Museum as it appeared in its new facilities at Ford's Theatre in 1932.

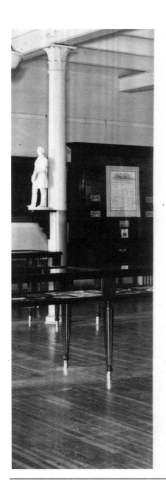

Lincoln memorabilia became a more refined museum about Lincoln's life; this in turn evolved into exhibits specific to the years of Lincoln's Presidency and his assassination. The 1968 installation in the newly built basement museum was presented in a more systematic manner reflecting the national sorrow arising from President John F. Kennedy's assassination in 1963. The installation focused on Lincoln's life rather than his death, and did not address the story of his assassination at all.

However, public interest in President Lincoln and curiosity surrounding his death and the conspiracy behind it grew over time. Responding to this interest, the National Park Service closed the Lincoln Museum in 1988 for two years of remodeling and extensive exhibit and curatorial work. The resulting 1990 museum answered, for the first time, the disturbing questions surrounding Lincoln's assassination. The exhibits address five different themes: "The Temper of the Times," "The Lincoln Assassination and the Aftermath," "The Lincoln Family in the White House," "The Legacy of Lincoln," and "The History and the Restoration of Ford's Theatre."

This black suit, gloves, and boots were worn by Lincoln as he watched "Our American Cousin" on April 14, 1865, the night he was shot.

The centerpiece of the Lincoln Museum is a life-size figure of Lincoln clad in the clothes he was wearing when he was assassinated, his custom-made black overcoat, Booth's weapons, and the door to the State Box.

Artifacts in the Lincoln Museum at Ford's Theatre, such as Mary Lincoln's china, also reflect the times and lifestyle of the Lincolns.

Conclusion

When the booming cannons and the clattering rifles of the Civil War fell silent, President Lincoln stood taller than any other hero. For five days after General Robert E. Lee's surrender at Appomattox Court House, jubilant Northerners celebrated their victory and praised the steadfast leadership of their President. President Lincoln turned his thoughts to the hard task of reunion.

On the evening of April 14, 1865, an audience, including President Lincoln, gathered at Ford's Theatre for the final performance of a popular comedy, "Our American Cousin." However, this was just the beginning of a real life play, one that triggered a chain of events that has indelibly shaped the history of the United States. John Wilkes Booth, the ultimate villain in this real-life drama, shattered the tenuous calm with a final act of terrible violence. His shocking assassination of President Abraham Lincoln was the grand finale of the Civil War, but the beginning of a new act, still playing out on the American stage more than 135 years later.

Suddenly the nation was without the leader who had so tenaciously guided it through the most devastating war in American history. The enormity and suddenness of the loss almost immediately defined the murdered President as a martyr to the causes of Union and Emancipation. The nation poured out an unprecedented display of grief in honor of the fallen leader. The millions of slaves, freed by Lincoln's Emancipation Proclamation in 1863, lamented the loss of "Father Abraham," fearing an uncertain future without his protection and leadership. The black crepe of mourning shrouded the country.

The echoes of Booth's fateful gunshot still haunt Americans today. Historians continue to look for answers to the endless questions surrounding Lincoln the man, his administration, and his death. John Wilkes Booth, an enormously popular nineteenth-century actor, is remembered only for his final performance as Lincoln's assassin.

Live performances are staged once again in historic Ford's Theatre, but the power of the sobering drama enacted there in 1865 still pervades the building. Ford's Theatre, now a National Historic Site, stands amidst the bustling Capital City, a solemn reminder of the legacy of a great man and how a single event can change the course of history. Today, the restored theater and museum combine with a living stage for the performing arts in a symbol of hope in the values we share as a nation.

Index

Eastern National

Eastern National is a non-profit organization that provides quality educational products and services to the visitors to America's national parks and other public trusts. It is educational, functioning as part of the interpretive arm of the National Park Service (NPS). It is a business that acquires, produces and sells cultural material for the enjoyment of park visitors. It is philanthropic, using net profit to help fund the interpretive activities of the NPS. Eastern National operates bookstores in over 170 national parks and public lands and has donated over $77 million to the NPS since 1947.

For more information, visit www.easternnational.org and www.eParks.com.

Eastern National
470 Maryland Drive, Suite 1
Fort Washington, PA 19034
215-283-6900

National Park Service

The National Mall and Memorial Parks division of the National Park Service is responsible for more than 1,000 acres of some of the United States' most significant natural and cultural resources. These sites are cherished symbols of our nation, located in the core of the Nation's Capital.

Ford's Theatre National Historic Site preserves and displays more than 8,000 artifacts relevant to the assassination of President Abraham Lincoln. Park rangers are available at Ford's Theatre National Historic Site to answer questions, provide assistance, and lead guided tours.

For more information about the National Park Service, visit their website at www.nps.gov and for more information about Ford's Theatre National Historic Site, visit their webpage at www.nps.gov/foth or write:

Ford's Theatre NHS
511 10th Street NW
Washington, DC 20004
202-426-6924

Credits

1: *architectural drawings*: NPS; *theater interior*: P&HA, Carol Highsmith; **4, 5**: NPS, Ford's Theatre Archive; **6**: *church*: NPS, Ford's Theatre Archive; **6, 7**: *10th Street*: Library of Congress; **8**: *campaign poster and buttons*: Lily Library, Indiana University; **9**: *campaign ticket and button*: P&HA, Carol Highsmith; **10**: *Walt Whitman*: Library of Congress; *eyeshields, brass knuckles, and ticket*: P&HA, Carol Highsmith; **11**: *political cartoons (left)*: NPS, Ford's Theatre Archive; *(right)*: Lily Library, Indiana University; **12**: *standing Lincoln*: Library of Congress; *portrait*: National Archives; **13**: *standing Mary Lincoln*: Library of Congress; *portrait*: NPS, Ford's Theatre Archive; **14**: NPS, Ford's Theatre Archive; **15**: *Lincoln Children*: NPS, Ford's Theatre Archive; **16**: Granger Collection; **17**: NPS, Ford's Theatre Archive; **18**: Library of Congress; **20**: *engravings*: Kiplinger Washington Collection; **21**: *beef depot engraving*: Library of Congress; *background and lower engraving*: Kiplinger Washington Collection; **22**: *playbills*: Library of Congress; **23**: *John and James Ford portraits and theatre*: NPS, Ford's Theatre Archive; **24**: *painting*: U. S. Senate Collection; *Emancipation Proclamation*: National Archives; **25**: *slavery engraving and handbill*: Library of Congress; **26**: *architectural drawings*: NPS; *fire background*: Photodisc; **27**: National Archives; **28**: *both images*: Maryland Historical Society, Baltimore, MD; **29**: *architectural drawings*: NPS; **30**: *keys and state box*: P&HA, Carol Highsmith; **31**: NPS, Ford's Theatre Archive; **32**: *parade of troops*: Library of Congress; **33**: *painting*: NPS, Antietam National Battlefield; **34**: *H. Greeley*: Library of Congress; **35**: *map*: from *The Civil War: The Assassination*, photograph by Edward Owen, © 1987 Time Life, Inc.; *war map book*: P&HA, Carol Highsmith; **36**: *U. S. Grant*: Library of Congress; *flags*: P&HA, Chuck Wasson; **37**: *R. E. Lee*: Library of Congress; **38**: *O'Dea painting*: NPS, Andersonville National Historic Site: *below*: Fort Ward Museum, Alexandria, VA; **39**: *engraving*: Fort Delaware Society; **40, 41**: *Arnold, Atzerodt, Herold, Powell, O'Laughlin*: Library of Congress; *cuffs, key*: P&HA, Carol Highsmith; *Mary Surratt*: courtesy of Surratt House Museum, M-NCPPC; **42**: The Harvard Theatre Collection, The Houghton Library; **43**: *Anderson Cottage*: Martin Luther King Library; **44**: *inauguration*: Granger Collection; *reception*: Kiplinger Washington Collection; **45**: *upper and lower*: Library of Congress; **46**: NPS, Ford's Theatre Archive; **47**: *inset*: NPS, Ford's Theatre Archive; *Jefferson Davis*: Museum of the Confederacy, Richmond, VA; **49**: P&HA, Carol Highsmith; **50**: *Appomattox Court House*: Library of Congress; **51**: *news-paper clipping*: Martin Luther King Library; *tickets*: P&HA, Carol Highsmith; **52**: *play book*: P&HA, Carol Highsmith; *stage*: NPS, Ford's Theatre Archive; **53**: *photos and playbill*: NPS, Ford's Theatre Archive; *violin*: P&HA, Carol Highsmith; **54**: *engraving*: NPS, Ford's Theatre Archive; *derringer*: P&HA, Carol Highsmith; **55**: Library of Congress; **56**: *newspaper clipping*: Martin Luther King Library; **57**: *upper and lower*: NPS, Ford's Theatre Archive; **58**: NPS, Ford's Theatre Archive; **59**: *upper left and right*: NPS, Ford's Theatre Archive; *revolver*: P&HA, Carol Highsmith; **60**: P&HA, Carol Highsmith; **61**: *engraving*: Library of Congress; **62**: Library of Congress; **63**: *upper*: NPS, Ford's Theatre Archive; *lower*: Library of Congress; **64**: *upper and lower*: Library of Congress; **65**: *upper*: NPS, Ford's Theatre Archive; *lower left*: National Archives; *lower right*: NPS, Ford's Theatre Archive; **66**: *funeral procession*: Library of Congress; *lower engraving and photo*: Library of Congress; *inset*: Illinois State Historical Society; **67**: *photo*: Library of Congress; **68**: *photo*: Library of Congress; **69**: *upper*: NPS, Ford's Theatre Archive; *map*: P&HA, Eve Hess; **70**: *photo*: Library of Congress; **71**: *artifacts*: P&HA, Carol Highsmith; *Mary Lincoln*: NPS, Ford's Theatre Archive; **72**: P&HA, Carol Highsmith; **73**: *compass*: from *The Civil War: The Assassination*, photograph by Edward Owen, © 1987 Time Life, Inc.; *map*: P&HA, Barbara Cross; **74**: *upper*: NPS, Ford's Theatre Archive; *lower*: courtesy of Surratt House Museum, M-NCPPC; **75**: *artifacts*: P&HA, Carol Highsmith; **76**: NPS, Ford's Theatre Archive; **77**: Library of Congress; **79**: *upper images*: NPS, Ford's Theatre Archive; **80**: *upper images*: NPS, Ford's Theatre Archive; *artifacts*: P&HA, Carol Highsmith; **81**: *upper*: NPS, Ford's Theatre Archive; *Mudd House*: Michael Kauffman; **82, 83**: P&HA, Carol Highsmith; **84**: *left*: Maryland Historical Society; *right*: National Archives; **85**: Lincoln National Life Foundation; **86**: NPS, Ford's Theatre Archive; **87**: *upper*: P&HA, Carol Highsmith; *lower photos*: NPS, Ford's Theatre Archive; **88**: *upper*: NPS, Ford's Theatre Archive; *lower*: P&HA, Carol Highsmith; **89**: *photos and architectural drawing*: NPS, Ford's Theatre Archive; **90**: *photos and architectural drawings*: NPS, Ford's Theatre Archive; **91**: P&HA, Carol Highsmith; **92**: Ford's Theatre Society; **93**: *playbills and photos*: Ford's Theatre Society; **94**: Library of Congress; **95**: *upper*: NPS, Ford's Theatre Archive; *lower*: Library of Congress; **96**: *artifacts*: from *The Civil War: The Assassination*, photograph by Edward Owen, © 1987 Time Life, Inc.; **97**: *upper image and lower artifacts*: P&HA, Carol Highsmith; **98, 99**: Ford's Theatre Society; **102**: Carol Diehl.

A. Lincoln: His Last 24 Hours. W. Emerson Reck. Jefferson, NC: McFarland and Company, 1987.

April '65. William A. Tidwell. Kent, OH: Kent State University Press, 1995.

Beware the People Weeping: Public Opinion and the Assassination of Abraham Lincoln. Thomas Reed Turner. Baton Rouge and London: Louisiana State University Press, 1982.

Come Retribution: The Confederate Secret Service and the Assassination of Lincoln. William A. Tidwell, James O. Hall and David Winfred Gaddy. Jackson and London: University of Mississippi Press, 1988.

Dr. Samuel A. Mudd and the Lincoln Assassination. John E. McHale, Jr. Parsippany, NJ: Billon Press, 1995.

The Escape and Capture of John Wilkes Booth. Ed Steers. Gettysburg, PA: Thomas Publications, 1992.

The Great American Myth. George S. Bryan, New York: Carrick Evans, 1940. Reprinted, Chicago: Americana House, 1990.

Lincoln: An Illustrated Biography. Philip B. Kunhardt, Jr., Philip B. Kunhardt III, and Peter W. Kunhardt, New York: Alfred A. Knopf, 1993.

The Lincoln Murder Conspiracies. William Hanchett, Urbana and Chicago: University of Illinois Press, 1983.

Right or Wrong, God Judge Me: The Writings of John Wilkes Booth. John Wilkes Booth, Louise Taper, John Rhodehamel, Champaign: University of Illinois Press, 1997.

Twenty Days: A Narrative in Text and Pictures of the Assassination of Abraham Lincoln. Dorothy Meserve Kunhardt and Philip B. Kunhardt, Jr. New York: Harper and Row, 1965. Reprinted, N. Hollywood, CA: Newcastle Publishing, 1985.

We Saw Lincoln Shot, Timothy S. Good, Jackson: University Press of Mississippi, 1995.

4ᵀᴴ FLOOR ELEV. 60 4 5

3ᴿᴰ FLOOR ELEV. 50 4 5

2ᴺᴰ FLOOR ELEV. 39 4 5

1ˢᵀ FLOOR ELEV. 30 N° 2
FIN. GRADE, SIDEWALK 1865

3ᴿᴰ FLOOR
ELEV. 60.5 5

2ᴺᴰ FLOOR ELEV. 44.5 5

1ˢᵀ FLOOR
ELEV.
29 4 5

NORTH WING

THEATRE BUILDING

WEST ELEVATION

DRAWN BY WM A DENNIN

UNDER DIRECTION OF UNITED STATES DEPARTMENT OF THE INTERIOR
NATIONAL PARK SERVICE, BRANCH OF PLANS AND DESIGN

511 TENTH STREET NORTHWEST

NAME OF STRUCTURE
FORD'S THEATRE

PLATE VIII